LEAPS
TRADING
STRATEGIES

Powerful Techniques
for Options
Trading Success

MARTY KEARNEY

WILEY

John Wiley & Sons, Inc.

Published by John Wiley & Sons, Inc., Hoboken, New Jersey
Published simultaneously in Canada

For general information about our other products and services, please contact our Customer Care Department within the United States at (800) 762-2974, outside the United States at (317) 572-3993 or fax (317) 572-4002.

Wiley publishes in a variety of print and electronic formats and by print-on-demand. Some material included with standard print versions of this book may not be included in e-books or in print-on-demand. If this book refers to media such as a CD or DVD that is not included in the version you purchased, you may download this material at http://booksupport.wiley.com. For more information about Wiley products, visit www.wiley.com.

ISBN 978-1-592-80343-9

Printed in the United States of America

10 9 8 7 6 5 4 3 2 1

Table of Contents
LEAPS Trading Strategies

PUBLISHER'S PREFACE

What you have in your hands is more than just a book. A map is simply a picture of a journey, but the value of this book extends well beyond its pages. The beauty of today's technology is that when you own a book like this one, you own a full educational experience. Along with this book's author and all of our partners, we are constantly seeking new information on how to apply these techniques to the real world. The fruit of this labor is what you have in this educational package; usable information for today's markets. Watch the video, take the tests, and access the charts—FREE. Use this book with the online resources to take full advantage of what you have before you.

If you are serious about learning the ins and outs of trading, you've probably spent a lot of money attending lectures and trade shows. After all the travel, effort, expense, and jet lag, you then have to assimilate a host of often complex theories and strategies. After thinking back on what you heard at your last lecture, perhaps you find yourself wishing you had the opportunity to ask a question about some terminology, or dig deeper into a concept.

You're not alone. Most attendees get bits and pieces out of a long and expensive lineage of lectures, with critical details hopefully sketched out in pages of scribbled notes. For those gifted with photographic memories, the visual lecture may be fine; but for most of us, the combination of the written word and a visual demonstration that can be accessed at will is the golden ticket to the mastery of any subject.

Marketplace Books wants to give you that golden ticket. For over 15 years, our ultimate goal has been to present traders with the most straightforward, practical information they can use for success in the marketplace.

Let's face it, mastering trading takes time and dedication. Learning to read charts, pick out indicators, and recognize patterns is just the beginning. The truth is, the depth of your skills and your comprehension of this profession will determine the outcome of your financial future in the marketplace.

This interactive educational package is specifically designed to give you the edge you need to master this particular strategy and, ultimately, to create the financial future you desire.

To discover more profitable strategies and tools presented in this series, visit www.traderslibrary.com/TLEcorner.

As always, we wish you the greatest success.

Chris Myers
President and Owner
Marketplace Books

HOW TO USE THIS BOOK

The material presented in this guide book and online video presentation will teach you profitable trading strategies personally presented by Marty Kearney and the Options Institute Council. The whole, in this case, is truly much greater than the sum of the parts. You will reap the most benefit from this multimedia learning experience if you do the following.

▶ WATCH THE ONLINE VIDEO

The online video at www.traderslibary.com/TLEcorner brings you right into Kearney's session, which has helped traders all over the world apply his powerful information to their portfolios. Accessing the video is easy; just log on to www.traderslibrary.com/TLEcorner, click *Leaps Trading Strategies: Powerful Techniques for*

Options Trading Success by Marty Kearney under the video header, and click to watch. If this is your first time visiting the Education Corner, you will be asked to create a username and password. It is all free with the purchase of this book and will be used when you take the self-tests at the end of each chapter. The great thing about the online video is that you can log on and watch the instructor again and again to absorb his every concept.

READ THE GUIDE BOOK

Dig deeper into Kearney's tactics and tools as this guide book expands upon his video session. Self-test questions, a glossary, and key points help ground you in this knowledge for real-world application.

TAKE THE ONLINE EXAMS

After watching the video and reading the book, test your knowledge with FREE online exams. Track your exam results and access supplemental materials for this and other guide books at www.traderslibrary.com/TLEcorner.

GO MAKE MONEY

Now that you have identified the concepts and strategies that work best with your trading style, your personality, and your current portfolio, you know what to do—go make money!

MEET MARTY KEARNEY

Marty Kearney is widely respected in the investing world as an expert on options and derivatives. As a senior instructor with the Options Institute for over 12 years, he has taught thousands of individual traders, exchange members, trading desks, and hedge funds on the many uses of options.

Marty spent years testing his ideas, perfecting his skills while trading for his own account, and communicating his successful techniques through classes and online instructional programs offered by the Options Institute.

Marty has a varied background. He was the marketing director for the NCR Corporation in the 1970s before joining the Chicago Board Options Exchange (CBOE). Today, he is the senior staff instructor of the Options Institute, the educational arm of the

CBOE. He became an independent market maker in 1981. Eleven years later he co-founded PTI Securities, a CBOE member firm. There, Marty implemented hedging strategies based on the use of listed options. He also authored PTI's weekly strategies letter for four years and composed the daily comments appearing on the PTI website. During his four years with PTI, he remained a part-time trader on the floor.

Marty is a regular contributor to a range of news services and industry publications, including Reuter's, CNBC, Bloomberg, CBS Radio Network, Barron's, *Fortune, Ticker Magazine*, and *Stock Futures and Options*. He has written for *Derivatives Week* and has appeared on many television programs. In addition to serving as an industry spokesman, Marty helps brokers develop new business using conservative options strategies. He is co-author of the successful book, *Understanding LEAPS*, and was a contributing author to *Options: Essential Concepts and Strategies* (3rd Ed.). He has served on many CBOE committees, including the Arbitration Committee (1984 to 1996).

Marty's educational background includes a BS from Saint Mary's University of Minnesota. He also pursued his MBA at Lake Forest Graduate School of Management. In 2006, he completed a three-year SII/SIA program at the Wharton School of the University of Pennsylvania.

In addition to his duties at the CBOE, Marty is also an instructor for the Options Industry Council (OIC). The OIC is an options educational organization backed by all the U.S. exchanges and the Options Clearing Corporation (OCC).

Introduction

Profits from LEAPS Options

The essential advantage of trading options is derived from the idea described by the old adage, "there are many ways to skin a cat." Novice traders are aware of one primary approach to investing: buying stock, holding it until it gains value, and then selling for a profit. While this basic approach does not always work out as planned, it is the inevitable starting point.

> The traditional buy-and-hold strategy is a fine starting point; but there is a lot more to the question of portfolio management. That is where options and LEAPS become so interesting.

Soon after diving into basic trading, they hear about "going short" or "speculating in futures," two ideas most novice traders believe increase risk. They might be attracted to mutual funds or exchange traded funds to diversify their risks and let someone else make the actual decisions.

Through the process of deciding how to expand beyond the basic strategy of buying-holding-selling shares of stock, they will eventually hear about options.

To some, options look like a craps table, with so many ways to play a throw of the dice. And in some respects, especially the highest-risk options strategies, it is a crap shoot. Looking at options in that light, however, misses the big picture. Options offer a broad spectrum of possibilities, and the many ways that people can use them—especially long-term or LEAPS options—can improve portfolio management, increase cash income, and reduce risks. I like using LEAPS options as part of a comprehensive and broad portfolio management strategy and not as a speculative play on a wild throw of the dice. Believe me, there are a variety of ways to use options, and you will see that many are designed to protect profits and help you grow capital.

THE RULES OF THE GAME

First, let's go over some basic rules of the game. Though options have been around in one form or another for several centuries, the modern era of options trading didn't begin until 1973, when standardized equity options were first introduced by the Chicago Board Options Exchange (CBOE). At that time, contracts were available on less than three dozen stocks, and trading was conducted in crowded pits by shouting floor brokers using hand signals and paper confirmation slips. Today, standardized options are available on roughly 2,800 stocks, 800 ETFs, and 200 indices; the average daily volume in 2007 was 11.4 million contracts, 14.7 million in 2008. Well over 90 percent of those transactions are done electronically, with orders matched by computer and trades completed in a matter of seconds.

In other words, thanks to increased experience, improved computer technology, and electronic market systems, option trading has become fast, efficient, and relatively low cost—even for individual investors. But for those who've had only limited exposure to options and the arenas in which they trade, we'll review some of the basics.

What exactly is an option? Though there are a few variations, the basic definition is this:

An option is a contract giving the buyer the right, but not the obligation, to buy or sell an underlying asset at a specific price on or before a certain date. An option is a security, just like a stock or bond, and constitutes a binding contract with strictly defined terms and properties.

As securities, options fall into a class known as derivatives. A derivative is a financial instrument that derives its value from the value of some other financial instrument or variable. For example, a stock option is a derivative because it derives its value from the value of a specific stock. An index option is a derivative because it derives its value from its relationship to the value of a specific market index, such as the S&P 500. The instrument from which a derivative derives its value is known as its underlying asset.

With options, there are two basic types (or classes)—calls and puts. Both are intangible contracts with a limited life. They expire at some point in the future, and after they expire, they are considered worthless.

> There are two kinds of options—calls and puts. The differences between the two are very important to remember as you study this industry.

A call grants its owner the right, but not the obligation, to buy 100 shares of a specified stock (the underlying security) at a fixed price. That option can be exercised at any time between the purchase of the call and its expiration, regardless of how high the stock's market value moves. As a rule, purchasers of call options are bullish; they expect the underlying stock's price to rise in the period leading up to the option's specified expiration date. Conversely, sellers of calls are usually bearish; they expect the price of the underlying stock to fall—or, at least, remain stable—prior to the option's expiration. However, there may be other reasons for selling calls, such as the structuring of strategies like spreads or covered writing.

A put is the opposite of a call. It grants its owner the right, but not the obligation, to sell 100 shares of a specified stock (the underlying security) at a fixed price. The put can be exercised at any time between purchase and expiration, no matter how low the price of the stock falls. Buyers of put options are generally bearish because they expect the price of the underlying stock to fall prior to the option's stated expiration date. Conversely, sellers of puts are usually bullish; they expect the price of the underlying stock to rise—or at least remain stable—through the option's expiration date. However, there might be other reasons for selling puts based on the objectives of certain strategies, such as lowering the cost basis on an intended, eventual purchase of the underlying stock.

Before you continue reading this book, make sure that the essential differences between calls and puts and how they work are firmly planted in your mind.

If you keep in mind the distinction between the two kinds of options as you read ahead, you will be able to better appreciate the development of the strategic plans I am going to present. These important differences are summarized in Table I.

Table I - Rights and Obligations		
	Calls	**Puts**
Buyers (holders)	RIGHT to buy	RIGHT to sell
Sellers (writers)	OBLIGATION to sell	OBLIGATION to buy

YOUR GOALS HELP DETERMINE YOUR CHOICE OF STRATEGIES

As noted earlier, options are among the most versatile of investment vehicles. They can be used for the most aggressive of speculations, and for purely defensive purposes. They can be used to produce large one-time profits, or to generate a steady stream of income. They can be used in the riskiest of investment pursuits, or specifically to insure against risk. They can be used when markets rise, when they fall, or when they fail to move at all. They can be used by themselves, in conjunction with other options of the same or different type, in combination with their underlying securities, and even with groups of essentially unrelated stocks.

In fact, there are at least a score of distinct investment strategies using options alone—and another dozen or so using options in association with other securities or underlying assets. So, how do you select the right strategy?

Obviously, the goals you hope to achieve using options will dictate the strategies you employ. If you expect a major market move and your desire is to reap maximum speculative profits, then you'll likely pick the simplest and most direct of the option strategies: the outright purchase of a put or call, depending on your views about the direction of the move.

If you expect a more modest price move but still want to seek speculative profits, then you might take a more conservative approach, choosing a vertical spread with either puts or calls, again depending on whether you are bullish or bearish. If you expect a major price move but aren't sure about the direction, you may opt to position one of the more exotic strategies, such as a straddle or strangle. If you own a stock and need to generate more income from your holdings, you might add an option to the mix and write a covered call. Or, if you own a large selection of stocks and want to protect yourself against a market downturn, you could choose to buy puts on a broad-based stock index.

In short, the strategic possibilities—like the potential profits offered by options—are virtually unlimited. Whatever your specific goal, you can likely find a way to achieve it using options, assuming, of course, you are correct in your assessment of what the underlying market is going to do and that you structure your option strategy properly.

EXPECT A LEARNING CURVE

In my experience, options are not a fast road to speculative riches but a way to enhance profits and make a portfolio safer. Perhaps more than anything else, LEAPS options are attractive because they last longer than the traditional listed option. This gives you more time for the kinds of important strategies we are going to consider here. These strategies include hedging other positions, insuring paper profits, or taking profits without having to sell stock. If those ideas sound promising, they are.

However, expect a learning curve—options can be complex. The jargon of the industry turns off many would-be options traders, and for those concerned with risk, the possibility of making an expensive mistake has frightened away many more. Just remember a few guidelines and you will be fine.

- Remember the distinction between calls and puts.

- Always consider whether a strategy is high-risk or low-risk; LEAPS strategies come in many flavors.

- If you are not sure about a strategy, never make a trade; wait until you understand it fully.

I promise you that if you read through my arguments and examples, you will find the world of LEAPS intriguing as well as manageable. Although the jargon and variety of choices can be daunting, by the time you are through with this book, you will understand how LEAPS options work. More important, you will have a good idea of how you can use the LEAPS strategies as part of your own portfolio.

Chapter 1

A BRIEF REVIEW OF
THE BASICS

I want to begin by going through the primary attributes of the LEAPS option, and explain how these are distinguished from better-known listed options.

If you read the introduction, then you're already familiar with the rules of the game: calls and puts. Now we need to cover the basics of all options. These concepts and definitions are mandatory before we proceed, so let's get started.

LEAPS is an acronym for **L**ong-term **E**quity **A**ntici**P**ation **S**ecurities.

IMPORTANT TERMS

Before proceeding to a discussion of LEAPS strategies, there are a few terms that are important to master.

- Strike price
- Exercise/Assignment
- Premium
- Expiration

Strike Price

The first and most distinguishing feature of LEAPS options is the strike price. Every option is an intangible contract granting rights to buyers and placing obligations on sellers. All of the valuation of those terms, and ultimately of the LEAPS option itself, are based on the strike price, the level at which the contract takes effect.

> Every LEAPS has a fixed strike price—the price at which the call or put can be exercised.

Every option is specifically related to an underlying security, usually a stock, ETF, or index. For example, if you buy Wal-Mart calls, they cannot be transferred to JCPenney or Sears. They are, and will always be, Wal-Mart calls. Strike price is the price per share at which that option can be exercised. As an example, let's say that you purchase an XYZ January 40 call at $2.25. If XYZ goes to $60 per share, the 40 strike call is $20 in-the-money (ITM). When an option is *in-the-money*, the current price of the underlying stock is higher than a call's strike price, or lower than a put's strike price. If XYZ fell to $30 per share, the 40 strike call would be considered $10 out-of-the-money (OTM). An option is *out-of-the-money* when the current price of the underlying stock is lower than a call's strike price, or higher than a put's strike price.

Exercise/Assignment

When an owner exercises a call, he or she is able to buy 100 shares at the strike price, even if current market value is much higher. When an owner exercises a put, he or she is able to sell 100 shares at the strike price, even if the current market value is far lower.

ITM LEAPS options can also be exercised (by owners of the options) or assigned (to investors who have sold the option) before expiration. This happens rarely, as long-term options usually have time premium embedded in the options price. When options are exercised, the Options Clearing Corporation assigns the exercised option to one of those sellers, either on a first-in, first-out basis or, usually, on a random basis.

Premium

The price of an option is called the premium. It is made up of two components, *intrinsic value* (how much the option is in-the-money) and *time premium* (the difference between the option price and its intrinsic value). If XYZ is trading at $60, and the 40 strike call is trading at $24 (the premium), $20 of that is intrinsic value and the other $4 is time premium. The further ITM the option goes, the greater the value of the option should be. Premium is the value per share, and because every option refers to 100 shares of stock, you have to read the quote properly. When you see that an option is worth 2, that means $200; if a LEAPS option is quoted at 4.35, its dollar value is $435.

The premium is the market value of the LEAPS, which rises and falls as the underlying security's value rises and falls, and as expiration nears.

Expiration

Another attribute of the LEAPS option is expiration. Every option expires at some point in the future. As expiration gets nearer, the likelihood of exercise increases as well, especially when the underlying security's market price is higher than the strike for calls, and when the underlying security's market value is lower than the strike for puts. Once the expiration date passes, all of the options pegged to that expiration cease to exist.

Distinctions also have to be made between LEAPS options and the more traditional, shorter-term listed options. First, LEAPS options exist up to 30 months, which is an incredibly long time when compared with the lifetime of eight months or so for non-LEAPS options. Because LEAPS options last beyond the current 12 months, the ticker symbols for LEAPS options are more complex than for traditional options. As dates get closer, specific strike prices and expiration times become more important. Overall, because of their longer-term option contracts, LEAPS offer a range of practical strategies.

So, let's sum up what we've learned about LEAPS so far:

- LEAPS are Long-term Equity AnticiPation Securities
- Can have a lifetime of up to 30 months (2 ½ years)
- Because of their length, they require different ticker symbols
- Many practical strategies can be applied to trading LEAPS

All LEAPS are going to expire in the future. Unlike shares of stock, which never expire, LEAPS have a limited life. This fact directly affects premium value.

DIFFERENCES: SECURITIES VERSUS OPTIONS

Although LEAPS share the same trading rules and attributes as traditional options, they are actually more like stocks. This is because they have lifetimes up to 30 months. The duration of a LEAPS contract is important because it is treated as a security (thus, the name Long-term Equity AnticiPation Security). But they are also conversion securities. This means that the closer the time gets to expiration (the third Friday of the expiration month/ year), the more a LEAPS starts to act like a traditional option. In their last nine months, LEAPS options behave more and more like traditional, shorter-dated options. This distinction is important only in an esoteric sense. As you will see later, strategies for trading LEAPS are really identical to those you would use for three, six, and nine month options, but the time frame is far longer. This provides you with more flexibility and often presents you with better pricing bargains and returns. Keep in mind, however, that LEAPS options—whether you think of them as securities or options—act like the old-style options and are used in the same ways to speculate, hedge, insure, or take profits on long positions.

 See that word "security"? LEAPS are not options, they are securities. To see this explained, log on to www. traderslibrary.com/TLEcorner.

A BRIEF HISTORY OF OPTIONS

The trading of standardized, listed options began in 1973 with the founding of the CBOE, the first U.S. options exchange[1]. In the beginning, these options used to be simple to track because their expiration month never exceeded a year. (Expiration month is the specific month when options expire.) So September options always expired the third Friday in September, and December options always expired the third Friday in December. Technically, it's the Saturday following the third Friday of the month, but "expiration friday" is the common usage.

As options gained popularity, it soon became apparent that both the floor traders and individual investors preferred to trade or hedge for shorter terms. So, the original rules were modified and

---

[1] Source: http://www.cboe.com/aboutcboe/History.aspx.

the CBOE decided that every stock would always have the current month plus the following month available to trade.

Every option you can think of now has options in the next two months as well as in their expiration cycle of three, six, and nine months. Every traditional option trades on one of three cycles: JAJO (January, April, July, October expirations); FMAN (February, May, August, November expirations); and MJSD (March, June, September, December expirations). So for listed options, you'll find contracts that expire in the next two months as well as those expiring in the coming months of their expiration cycles.

Expiration cycles and months used to be quite limited; today, option traders have more variety and flexibility, not only in the duration of options, but also in the frequency of expirations.

Then, traders asked: "Well, it's nice to be able to trade in the immediate one or two months, but if we can go out nine months, why can't we have a product that goes out further?" So LEAPS evolved to address that. On October 5, 1990, the CBOE introduced LEAPS to supply investors' demand for options with longer-term expirations. Because LEAPS appealed to both options and stock traders, they proved successful from the start[2].

Currently, on the U.S. exchanges that trade options, there are about 2,800 stocks on which you can trade options. Unfortunately, only

---

[2] Source: http://www.cboe.com/LearnCenter/Advanced.aspx#leaps.

about 900 of those stocks also offer LEAPS, so not every stock has long-term options. "What?" you might be asking. "Only one-third of the stocks have LEAPS? Which ones?" Well, the stocks that are in the news—the stocks that trade, such as IBM, Microsoft, QQQQ, and Intel, for example.

Today, LEAPS extend as far as approximately two and a half years. They can technically go out 39 months, but at this point, 30 months is the longest duration you will find.

OPTIONS SYMBOLS[3]

U.S. options trading symbols tell us four important things about the option: what the underlying stock is, whether the option is a call or a put, the option's expiration month and its strike price, all in just a few letters. To help you understand, let's break down an option ticker symbol into three parts.

- The first two to three letters of an option ticker make up the option symbol, which tells you what the underlying stock is for that particular option. Normally, this is the same as the stock symbol and is common to all options for that company, but there are exceptions. For example, Microsoft's stock symbol is MSFT, but MSQ and MFQ are both used as option symbols for the company.
- The single letter immediately following the option symbol tells you the option's expiration date and whether it is a call or a put. Since there are 12 possible expiration periods for

---

[3] Source: http://www.investopedia.com/ask/answers/05/052505.asp

options (one per month), letters A through L are used for calls, and letters M through X are used to represent puts.

- Finally, the last letter of an option ticker symbol corresponds with the specific strike price of that option.

STOCK SYMBOLS[4]

The New York Stock Exchange is the oldest stock exchange in America. Since that is where modern trading began, many of the companies listed on the NYSE have ticker symbols that consist of only one or two letters. Today, if a company's symbol consists of three letters, it is traded on either the NYSE or the AMEX. NASDAQ stocks generally have symbols consisting of four to five letters. However, in July 2007, the U.S. Securities and Exchange Commission began allowing companies that transfer listings from other exchanges to the NASDAQ to keep their ticker symbols, regardless of the number of letters.

Originally, with traditional options, there was only one September contract and one December contract. A two-digit designation was added to the end of the option quote—one for the month and another for the strike. There are only 12 months, so the alphabet worked well for that. If you use five-point increments, there are only 20 possible strike prices in a 100-point range, so the alphabet worked for that as well. Thus, before LEAPS came along, you could look at a ticker symbol such as WMT FJ and say, "This is a Wal-Mart June

---

[4] Source: http://www.money-zine.com/Investing/Stocks/Stock-Tickers-and-Ticker-Symbols and http://www.reuters.com/article/governmentFilingsNews/idUSN1036624820070710.

When options first started, the stocks being traded made it fairly simple. IBM's symbol was IBM and so on, with 3-letter symbols. But then Microsoft, MSFT, came along and its symbol was made MSQ and things began to get confusing. To hear Marty clarify "options symbology," watch at www.traderslibrary.com/TLEcorner.

(F is the sixth letter, representing the sixth month call) 50 (J is the tenth letter, times $5 increments, equals the 50 strike) call." Puts would use one of the 12 letters at the end of the alphabet. To this day, I bump into investors that say "I have a question about the WMT FJs," and they don't see my hand behind my back counting out the month and strike prices!

When LEAPS entered the market, the possibilities broadened to two or three contracts on a stock with the same strike price and the same month of expiration (a January 35 put for 2009, 2010 and 2011, for example). But the system could only accommodate expirations for one year. So, thanks in part to LEAPS, the system of trading symbols had to be expanded.

Table 1.1 - LEAPS - Ticker Symbols	
Wal-Mart	Stock symbol: WMT
	Regular Option symbol: WMT
	LEAPS Symbols: LWT('04) ZWT('05)
Microsoft	Stock symbol: MSFT
	Regular Option symbol: MSQ
	LEAPS Symbols: LMF('04) ZMF('05)

Today, every stock offering LEAPS uses a two-tier symbol. One is used for regular options, and the other for LEAPS. While other options have fixed symbols, LEAPS symbols change to reflect the expiration year. This is supposed to make it easier to distinguish a longer-term option from a shorter-term option in data listings. The letters L and Z were chosen to represent these "miscellaneous situations." For example, Wal-Mart is designated as WMT for its short-term options listings, and LWT or ZWT for LEAPS (see Table 1.1). This is confusing and complicated, but it is the system we have to live with—but not for long. Just as computer design in the 1950s failed to anticipate future complications by using only a two-digit year field, the designers of exchange symbols for option trading never anticipated the needs growing from expansion into LEAPS. But the need for an improved system of symbols is now apparent.

Unfortunately, the two-digit system for identifying options is not well-suited to today's expanded terms for LEAPS. A new and better system is on the way!

To make it even worse, we have also run out of symbols that start with the letter L and the letter Z. Now you'll see some option symbols on the ticker for LEAPS that start with O or K as well, just to help confuse you.

The need for an expanded system includes not only multiple year/month expirations, but also the possibility of prices spanning more than 100 points (or, at the very least, making LEAPS available in those different price ranges). In today's volatile market, the likelihood of a stock moving 100 points or more is the new reality. Anyone who has followed Google for the past few years knows that this can and does occur. So a GOOG 250 strike, 350, 450, 550, and 650 strikes would each need unique option symbols.

Symbology: What to Expect

We have discussed option symbology, how it was designed, and how unforeseen events critically compromised its effectiveness. Well, as the talented songwriter Bob Dylan once said, "The times, they are a-changin'."

Are you reading this before or after late February 2010? The reason I ask is the much-anticipated solution scheduled for the first quarter of 2010.

The final symbol project may change before the publication of this book, but some things that you can expect to see include:

- Four digit option symbols. QCOM will not be abbreviated to QAQ and permutations of that. They're leaving room for a six digit symbol.
- Strike prices in decimals, not fractions. Strike prices over 1,000, with three decimal places, allow for unusual stock splits.
- The day, month, and year of expiration. Expect to see something like the following in 2010: GOOG 1/20/2012 330 call 2.25

- Room to grow for interest rate options, flexible options (FLEX), currencies, volatility options, and others to follow. Good-bye WMT FJs!

MEANINGFUL STRIKES AND EXPIRATION STYLE

The range of possible strike prices for calls or puts over two to three years is substantial. A meaningful strike price can mean different things to people employing various strategies, but here's one important aspect to remember: the longer out the expiration goes, the more remote the final outcome. As a buyer, I have the right to exercise a LEAPS call or put any time I want. The potential is there, and this gives me great freedom. It means that for a relatively small cost, I can control 100 shares of stock for a long time. In the stock market, 30 months can define the difference between bull and bear markets. The entire situation for any one company is likely to be vastly different that far away. If I sell options, it is true that they could be exercised at any time, but what are the chances? The odds are quite remote, but it could happen; and this is one of the uncertainties sellers have to accept when they short a LEAPS position.

Investors know that they can move into and out of LEAPS options as they can with shorter-dated options. Whether they have a position in a stock (called an "equity" by professionals), an ETF (exchange traded fund) or an index, a contract can be closed at any time before expiration. Since LEAPS are longer-dated by definition, they may not be the best investment vehicle for a short-term outlook.

All stock and ETF options (and a few index options) are "American Style" options, which can be exercised or assigned at any time before expiration. Most index options are "European Style", meaning that one cannot exercise or be assigned before Expiration Friday. Most users of index options like this; the position stays on until they decide to exit it. Another important characteristic of index options is that they all settle in cash. IBM options settle in shares of IBM, while index options (DIA, for example) settle in cash.

The term "meaningful strike prices" was probably coined by a marketer years ago. With shorter-term IBM options for example, you might find July options with 110, 115, 120, 125, 130, and 135 strike prices. With LEAPS options, there might be IBM strike prices going out 20 to 30 months, but only with 110, 120, and 130 strike prices. Some of this has to do with the amount of strike prices (hundreds of thousands) and the capability of disseminating all of the bids, offers, and last trades of each option. So to some of us, the term "meaningful strike prices" could also be called "slightly fewer but certainly significant strike prices to choose from." I guess "meaningful strike prices" does indeed sound better.

OPTIONS/LEAPS PRICING

When we talk about options or LEAPS pricing, we are still dealing with the basic components of these instruments:

- Stock price
- Strike price
- Time to expiration
- Interest rate / dividends
- Volatility

We need to ask: What's the stock price? What strike price are we looking at? How much time until expiration? What are the interest rates and dividends? Granted, dividends and interest rates with options having less than six months of life are considered the least important components if you are only trading the options, and not also owning shares of stock. But if you use long-term options (LEAPS), interest rates and dividends can have a more dramatic effect. For example, for LEAPS going out 25 or 30 months, the interest rate can be very significant.

We also have to judge trades based on the volatility of the underlying security. No two stocks will trade at the same volatility. They'll change like the waves in the ocean, varying with traders' and investors' expectations, as well as adjustments in supply and demand.

Using Options Requires More Decisions

Let's face it, using options requires more decisions. If you're going to buy IBM stock, you buy the stock; if you'd like to consider some IBM options, there are 250 different choices in any permutation of those buying and selling, as well as any particular spreading or combination of these options. At the very least, you need to be aware of (a) the range of possibilities, (b) the risk/reward scenario of each, and (c) how risk/reward is affected by proximity between market value and strike.

In the next chapter, I will address some of these questions by explaining why LEAPS are attractive alternatives to traditional option trading and the old "buy and hold" approach of just buying stocks and holding on to them, hoping they will grow in value over the years. The questions are more complex when LEAPS come into play, and of course, so are the answers.

SELF-TEST QUESTIONS

1. The strike price of a LEAPS option is:

    a. the current price of the underlying security, so-called because it is the level where a LEAPS trade "strikes."

    b. a value level of stock where it becomes possible to exercise a LEAPS, also called parity.

    c. the fixed price at which options may be exercised.

    d. the crossover point between traditional short-term listed options and extended expiration cycles of LEAPS.

2. Exercise is:

    a. the opposite term of assignment

    b. the act of taking delivery of stock at the fixed strike price by exercising a call

    c. the act of delivering stock at the fixed strike price by exercising a put

    d. all of the above

3. The premium is defined as:

    a. the current market value of a LEAPS.

    b. extra payment made to buy LEAPS with greater than average potential to rise in value.

    c. profits earned through the exercise of a LEAPS option, apart from capital gains and dividend income.

    d. the combination of LEAPS profits and dividends, excluding capital gains on the underlying security.

4. The abbreviation FMAN stands for:

    a. Future Merger & Acquisition Numerator (a contingent valuation model for options in companies that are takeover candidates).

    b. February, May, August, November, an expiration cycle.

    c. Feb-Mar-Apr Numerator (part of a valuation model for short-term options).

    d. Fiscal Marketing Assessment & Numeration (the procedure employed by U.S. exchanges for setting option premium values).

5. LEAPS are available on:

    a. about one-third of U.S. listed companies.

    b. all listed companies.

    c. all listed companies offering traditional options.

    d. only the 30 industrials in the Dow.

For answers, go to www.traderslibrary.com/TLEcorner.

Chapter 2

WHY BOTHER WITH LEAPS?

Why would you trade long-term instruments (LEAPS) when you could trade shorter-term, lower-priced options? The answer is a good one: that longer term—up to three years compared to only a few months—makes so many option and LEAPS strategies more practical and more effective.

As you can see in Figure 2.1, the time decay of LEAPS is substantially different from short-term options. All of the U.S. exchanges have approved the slope of LEAPS time decay. Approval has also been granted by the compliance department of the Options Industry Council (OIC). A few years ago, a particular LEAPS contract did not show dramatic movement in time decay in those first couple of years, and the line had to be altered. The slope had to be

FIGURE 2.1- LEAPS Time Decay

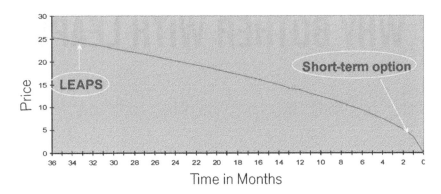

Time in Months

*$100 stock, 100-strike call, 30% vol, 5% interest rate, no divs.

Source - OIC

made much more dramatic. But the idea here is that options do not decay in a linear manner.

 Options decay at the square root of time. To see this explained, log on to www. traderslibrary.com/TLEcorner.

If a one-month option is trading at one, the four-month option is not trading at four. There is a lot of variation, and you have to expect it. The volatility of the underlying stock is going to affect how time value falls. In fact, you could separate out the pure, rather predictable time element, and then view the variations as a volatility premium. That is usually called extrinsic value, to distinguish the price movement patterns from pure time value.

> Option value does not move predictably because time is only part of the equation. Volatility is also a factor, and the further out expiration is, the less the LEAPS premium reacts to stock price changes.

GETTING TIME, DOING TIME

Here's an anecdote about how options work: one of our Options Institute instructors was in an elevator a few years ago, taking some friends out to lunch. In the back of the elevator were a few people from our compliance department, who have to approve everything we put together and talk about to the public. How did our instructor know that's who they were? Well, because they were wearing the pencil protectors on their shirt, a sure sign. And I don't mean that as an affront to anyone; it's simply the truth.

The instructor decides to have a little fun with these compliance folks, so he says to them, "Listen, we're thinking of doing a new seminar pretty soon." The compliance people looked at each other and one asked, "Well, can you send us the material? We'll carve it up and make the changes and additions and deletions that are required." The instructor's friends knew that these people were already on the hook. He had them, but they didn't know where this was leading. He said, "Yeah, we're thinking of doing a seminar on buying call options." So the compliance guy repeated, "Well, send us the material; we'll take a look at it."

The instructor added, "We're thinking of doing a seminar on buying call options for prisoners. Why? Well, because doesn't it seem like time passes very quickly when you own options?" The compliance people repeated the same mantra, "Well, send us the material. We'll take a look at it." So he said, "Well, if you're going to be that way about it, forget it." It's funny how quickly time goes by when you own options.

> Don't forget the Theory of Relativity. When you have open option positions, time flies, and not always in a good way.

Many traders have owned options at some point or another where there just wasn't enough time. I have owned options that expired on Friday, and the company was taken over the following Sunday. Why not give ourselves more time? If the one-month option is trading for $1, the two-month option might be trading somewhere around $1.50. The three-month option might be trading at about $1.75. Rather than buy the two-month option for $1.50, why not buy 50% more time for $.25? This is the idea of using time to your advantage.

If you expand that out, why not buy a one-year or two-year option? For that much more time, the incremental cost is not that bad and you can buy yourself more time to make a profitable event happen. With the traditional, short-term listed option, not only do you have to be right about what direction the underlying stock is going, you have to fit it into a short time frame. That's why LEAPS are such a great product; they let you think long-term instead of having to calculate whether a particular profit event can occur within a few months or a few weeks.

> The LEAPS advantage is that it allows time for your strategic plan to develop. That is not always possible with traditional options that only have a few months of time before expiration.

ACTION, REACTION – ANOTHER LEAPS BENEFIT

Let's look at an example that chooses between a short-term option and a LEAPS option. Table 2.1 shows a $50 stock; so let's take a look at the 50 strike price call option. We're bullish on the stock. Rather than buy that one or two-month option, let's buy the three-month option.

I'm not limited to the short-term options, however. I could buy the two-year LEAPS option and risk $11. If I own the LEAPS, I have much more at risk, don't I?

Maybe not. Let's see what happens. If after one month, the stock doesn't move and is still at 50, we're still looking at the 50 strike price call. As we say on the trading floor, the stock is sharply un-

Table 2.1- LEAPS Time Erosion	3-mo option	2-yr LEAP
Now:	3.40	11.00
1 month later:	2.75	10.70
2 months later:	1.90	10.40
3 months later:	0	10.10
*stock unchanged @ $50 / 50 strike calls		

changed. How do these options react? Well, it's pretty simple. We could buy the LEAPS option out 2 years and pay $11, or we could buy the 3-month option eight times at $3.40 and risk $27.20. The second option works if we'd like to keep repeating the process every three months; buying that three-month option and hoping it becomes profitable. But this is not reasonable, because with rapid time decay the odds are against that happening. With the stock going nowhere, the short-term option loses approximately 65 cents over the first of the three months. One month later the stock is still trading at $50. Now what? The option loses about 85 cents, making it increasingly unlikely that you are going to be profitable in this position. There just isn't enough time.

> When expiration is close, a point drop is often a disaster, and recovery becomes less and less likely. You need more time.

What if you were to buy the two-month option? As the option approaches Expiration Friday and the stock is still trading at $50, that whole $1.90 is going to be lost. You can see how the decay accelerates as we approach Expiration Friday.

Compare that outcome to the alternative—buying a LEAPS option at the same strike price going out two years, or 24 months. How does it do? It only loses about 30 cents, or about 3%, that first month, even with the stock unchanged.

That second month, it loses another 30 cents or so. The third month it loses 30 cents (3%), taking its value down to $10.10. By owning the LEAPS option, we had about 90 cents of time decay. By own-ing that at-the-money short-term option with three months to go, we can lose the entire $3.40. This depicts time decay in a real world application with all of the particulars being the same: interest rates, dividends, volatility, or lack of volatility.

The point here is that the LEAPS alternative gives you more time because stock price movement often takes time to develop. In com-parison, time decay for options about to expire is going to be quite accelerated.

PROS AND CONS

It is worthwhile to compare the pros and cons of LEAPS over short-term options as a way to determine whether they are actually a sensible alternative. (See Table 2.2)

Pros
The advantages include the obvious lower cost per unit of time. You're spending money; but when you look at the cost over the

Table 2.2 - LEAPS Pros and Cons	
Pros	• Lower cost per unit of time
	• Less time erosion
	• Longer life, more time for a strategy to work
Cons	• Higher absolute cost
	• Lower sensitivity to change in stock price

two to three years remaining before expiration, it's not that bad. Just as important, with that much time remaining, you are going to experience less time erosion, at least until you get quite close to expiration, say within four or five months of the expiration date. Finally, the longer life of the LEAPS option gives you more time for a strategy to work, and that is the key. The big problem with traditional short-term options is that there is simply not enough time.

> The exchange you accept with LEAPS options is simple. You buy more time and, in exchange, you pay more money.

Cons

There are also disadvantages, of course. First, there is the cost. The absolute cost is always higher because you have to pay for that time—the longer the time remaining, the higher the absolute cost. It's a good news/bad news scenario. No option strategy offers a benefit without a corresponding cost or potential drawback. You are likely to give up something on the other side. Cost is one example. You get a lot of time, but you have to pay for it. Study the listings for any series of options and you will see what I mean. Cost goes up as time to expiration is extended into the future.

The second major disadvantage is that LEAPS contracts have lower sensitivity to price movement. With short-term options, you expect to see a tracking trend. So stock price moves and option premium follows, and as expiration approaches, this trend becomes absolute. Because the time value is close to zero, all of the movement is intrinsic as long as your option is in-the-money.

That lower price sensitivity is an advantage in some respects. If the stock isn't moving or if its value is falling, the LEAPS is not likely to react, especially not as much as the short-term option. But on the other side of this, if you own a long call, you are not going to see a lot of profit right away. The stock might rise five points, but depending on the strike price chosen, the LEAPS call might only move a point or two.

In technical lingo, we would say that the LEAPS option has a much lower delta (For the definition of *delta*, see page 43). And with a short-term option, the rate of return on any profitable change is going to be much higher as well. For example, if you buy a three-month call and pay $3.40, a one dollar movement by expiration is a 29% return. A one dollar movement on an $11 LEAPS is only 9%.

Be Patient

A LEAPS option's value is less likely to respond to stock price movement because expiration is so far away. So if you expect a fast profit from LEAPS speculation, you have to remember that it takes time.

You need to weigh the advantages and disadvantages, of course. The LEAPS is going to yield a lower return if it costs you more to move into the long position; but, in exchange, you have a much longer time frame for the position to become profitable. Think about any $50 stock. Over the next three months, it is likely to move only a few points at most in either direction. There's just not much time. But how much can that stock move in two or three years? In the market, that is an eternity. If you have been following the market in the recent volatile times, you know that a lot can happen over two or three years. That's why LEAPS options are so exciting.

> Because LEAPS options cost more due to the longer time horizon, any net return is going to be lower than a less expensive, shorter-term option. This is another trade-off you give in exchange for the time advantages.

1. Time decay refers to:

   a. the decline in option value on the last trading day before expiration.

   b. a tendency for prices to fall by midday in any trading session that starts out on a strong upward trend.

   c. the loss of premium value over time.

   d. a tendency among traders to lose interest in an option series that remains available for too many months.

2. Based on the price at which a one-month option is selling:

   a. you can estimate mathematically exactly where all other options should be valued.

   b. long-term options are valued at a factor of 1 ¾ times per month.

   c. long-term options increase incrementally as time is extended, on a predictable curve.

   d. you cannot determine the value of long-term options, due to volatility variance and other factors.

3. The biggest problem with short-term options is:

    a.   there is not enough time for many strategies to develop.

    b.   they are always too expensive.

    c.   the rate of return is always far too low.

    d.   you cannot always find a buyer when you are ready to sell.

4. When the underlying stock does not change price:

    a.   a LEAPS option should have more premium value than a short-term option.

    b.   short-term options tend to lose premium value rapidly, due to pending expiration.

    c.   long-term strategies may still work out over time.

    d.   all of the above.

5. Among the advantages of LEAPS, you can expect:

    a.   fast resolution of strategies due to fast expiration schedules.

    b.   lower premium cost due to a general lack of interest among traders.

    c.   a lower cost per unit of time.

    d.   all of the above.

For answers, go to www.traderslibrary.com/TLEcorner.

Chapter 3

USING LEAPS IN A GIFTING PROGRAM

Let's consider how you can use LEAPS options in a gifting program. For example, let's say you want to give $30,000 to a grandchild or other relative, and you plan to gift $10,000 per year over the next three years.

The obvious way to do this would be to buy $30,000 worth of stock now, with plans to sell it off and donate one-third cash each year, or to transfer the stock if that is part of the plan. The big question, of course, is whether or not LEAPS can be used to target your objective.

One of the reasons I am using $10,000 for this example has to do with gift taxes. As the tax laws currently stand (and there is talk of revising the following dollar amount slightly higher), as long as you are at or below the $10,000 level, you can make the gift tax-free. But if you give more than $10,000, you have to pay a federal gift tax. Yes, you, the gift giver, are taxed if your gift is higher than $10,000 per year per person. So you and your spouse can each gift $10,000 to the same person, or you can give $10,000 each to three grandchildren.

> Remember, you as gift giver are taxed if your gift to any one person is higher than $10,000 per year.

So LEAPS could be an interesting option if you think today's stock price is attractive but you want to avoid going over that $10,000 level. You don't want to give away $30,000 all in the same year because that will cost you gift tax.

THE THREE-YEAR PLAN

Here is a plan that allows you to work with stock at its current price, plan out three years, and use LEAPS to achieve what you need. What steps would you need to take? Let's start with Table 3.1.

The stock is trading right now at $39 per share. In this example, I am using the January 2011 LEAPS call with a strike price of 30. These are in-the-money by nine points and are trading at $14.

> By purchasing LEAPS instead of buying stock, you can control many more shares for a lower dollar amount.

Table 3.1 - **Using LEAPS in a Gifting Program**
• XYZ is currently trading at $39 per share
• The XYZ January 2011 LEAPS 30 call is trading at $14.
• Step 1?
• Step 2?
• Step 3?

Step 1: Today

You can invest $10,000 in the account of the person receiving your gift, and then buy seven of those January 30 calls. Remember, this assumes you have 30 months or so before expiration; so, this is a plan working from a premise of planning from about July 2008 and looking forward 30 months. In this case those $14 calls are going to cost $9,800, plus trading costs. Now consider what you have done. In this account, you control 700 shares of stock for the next two and a half years. (See Table 3.2)

Table 3.2 - **Using LEAPS in a Gifting Program - Step 1 : Today**
• Deposit $10,000 in recipient's account
• Buy 7 XYZ January 2011 30 LEAPS Calls at $14 each (Total Cost $9,800 + comm.)

Step 2: Next Three Years

Deposit additional sums of $10,000 in any month of the applicable calendar years. In our example, you can deposit these sums in any month of 2009 and 2010. Once all of the deposits have been made, you have donated $30,000 to the recipient's account. (See Table 3.3)

Table 3.3 - Using LEAPS in a Gifting Program - Step 2: Next Three Years	
2009 (any month)	Deposit $10,000 in recipient's account
2010 (any month)	Deposit $10,000 in recipient's account

When you make a gift, the $10,000 limit is calculated on a calendar-year basis. You can make a gift contribution in any month of the year.

Step 3: Above $30

This is where you make a few decisions concerning exercise.

Let's assume that the stock is trading above $30 per share. At any time, you can exercise the LEAPS calls. This allows you to buy at the fixed $30 per share price. Based just on your first year's contribution of $10,000, that lets you exercise and buy stock for $21,000. Remember, while this was going on, the money you had put aside for gifting was earning interest. One-third was earning interest for one year and one-third for two years, so you now have increased the base of the money available for gifting. Having that money available in the account gives you the cash to buy stock at the fixed price of $30, even though the stock is valued far higher. (See Table 3.4)

Table 3.4 - Using LEAPS in a Gifting Program - Step 3: Above $30
• XYZ above $30 in January 2011
• If still bullish on XYZ: exercise calls and purchase 700 XYZ at $30
• Total cost 700 x $30 = $21,000 + comm. ($20,200 in recipient's account, plus intrest)
• You can sell the calls if you wish. (Taxes?)

You can use the first year's contribution to buy LEAPS, and the second and third year contribution to convert to shares of stock.

So in this outcome, you contribute $30,000 over three years and spend $9,800 on calls. Two years later, you have accumulated an additional $20,000 in the account, taking the cash balance up to $20,200, plus interest. Exercising the seven calls at $30 is simple because the cash is there. It will cost $21,000, but that cash will be there because the funds have earned interest. Earning just 3% interest will cover this easily.

As a second choice, if you don't want to exercise the LEAPS calls, you can sell them. If your original idea—before considering LEAPS in the plan—was just to buy shares of stock for the recipient, that's all well and good. But what if the situation has changed and you no longer think buying stock is all that great an idea? You can sell the LEAPS calls.

Table 3.5 - Using LEAPS in a Gifting Program - Step 3: Below $30
• XYZ below $30 in January 2011
• Calls expire for a total loss of cost of calls.
• There is still $20,200-plus in recipient's account.

But, let's assume that the stock's price has fallen below $30 per share. Now it would make no sense to exercise because the strike price is $30. So you close the position by selling the original seven calls. You still have $20,200 in the account, plus accrued interest. Table 3.5 shows what happens if the call expires worthless.

> You don't have to exercise. You can also sell LEAPS calls and take a profit or a loss. The advantage is that you have many choices using LEAPS.

So here is the advantage: If you had bought shares of stock directly and the stock's price fell from $39 down to $10, you would have lost most of the money. But in this situation, where you spent $9,800 to get seven calls and you saw the stock's price fall, you would take a loss on the seven LEAPS calls, but still have that $20,200 in the account. You would keep two-thirds of your powder dry, right? In a highly volatile market, this kind of defensive planning makes a lot of sense. If the stock's price rises, you exercise and get an immediate profit because your basis in the stock will be below market value. If the stock's price falls, you cut your losses.

> As a defensive move, you can use LEAPS in volatile markets to minimize losses. Remember, in the market, three years is a very long time.

But how about this idea: let's suppose the shares of XYZ are trading at $10 as expiration in 2011 approaches. You think the sell-off in the shares of XYZ is over, and your recipient should participate in the expected stock movement higher. The expiring LEAPS calls of 2011 are set to expire worthless, but you have over $20,200 in the account. You could buy shares at $10, or you could buy seven of the LEAPS calls for 2013, leaving the balance of cash to earn interest for the next two years. (If you were thinking of purchasing the 2014 LEAPS calls, you had a good idea; but, they won't exist for the next 4-6 months, so 2013 is as far out in time as you can go).

There are some variations to this strategy. First, you could buy LEAPS calls for yourself and save the purchase price of the stock over two years. By purchasing LEAPS calls right at the beginning of this two-and-a-half-year process, you would end up saving money. This lets you pay for the stock later, if and when you exercise. In this way, you still control shares of stock for a relatively minimal investment. So when the value rises later, you exercise and convert your LEAPS calls into $10,000 worth of stock and present that as the gift.

Another way to accomplish the same thing is to use "found money" to buy LEAPS calls. This could be a year-end bonus, for example, or a tax refund.

The third variation is to buy LEAPS calls and deposit sufficient funds in a money market account. This limits your risk to the price of the calls—a good defensive move.

The point to remember with all of this is that a gifting program is not necessarily limited to a cash contribution or shares of stock. You can use LEAPS defensively in volatile markets, or you can set things up to use second and third-year donations to exercise LEAPS purchases if the stock's price rises. This enables you to develop the gifting program with considerable flexibility.

 There are ways to buy LEAPS now and figure out how to pay for them later. Find out how at www.traderslibrary.com/TLEcorner.

Self-test questions

1. In a gifting program:

   a. you have to use cash only under IRS requirements.

   b. the recipient has to pay gift taxes on any gifts exceeding $10,000 per year.

   c. the gift giver has to pay gift taxes on any gift exceeding $10,000 per year to any one gift recipient.

   d. there is no tax on the value of any gift.

2. Strategies under a gifting program may include:

   a. cash contributions.

   b. donations in shares of stock.

   c. purchased LEAPS.

   d. any of the above.

3. If you purchase LEAPS calls for a gift recipient:

   a. you have the advantage of being able to exercise or sell, based on future movement in the stock's price.

   b. you must convert those calls to shares of stock before expiration date.

   c. the strike price of the LEAPS must be higher than the current value of the stock.

   d. the strike price of the LEAPS must be lower than the current value of the stock.

4. If you buy LEAPS calls in the first year of a gifting program:

    a. you cannot use later year gifts to fund exercise.

    b. you are required to exercise with additional contributions above the annual $10,000 limit.

    c. you can use subsequent years' contributions to fund exercise of those LEAPS.

    d. you are banned from simply selling the LEAPS calls once you have given them as gifts.

5. If you spend gifted funds on LEAPS, and the stock price later falls below the LEAPS strike price:

    a. you must contribute additional funds to make up the loss in the account.

    b. you have the choice of selling the LEAPS calls at a loss.

    c. exercise is your best remaining choice.

    d. it creates a tax shelter for the gift recipient.

For answers, go to www.traderslibrary.com/TLEcorner.

Chapter 4

LEAPS VS. STOCK OWNERSHIP

Let me tell you an interesting story about LEAPS. When I was down on the trading floor as a market maker in the early 1990s, my exchange had a very interesting advertising campaign. This may have been the only advertising campaign I ever liked.

> Buying LEAPS instead of stock is a form of leasing as an alternative to buying.

The campaign was simple. It asked, "Why buy a stock if you can lease one?" Think about that. Why do people own stock? It's not to go to a party and say, "I've got 500 shares of Lucent." No, it's because you're investing in America and you think this particular investment is going up in value, right? You don't necessarily care what it is; you would just like to try to make money on it.

Maybe you've leased equipment before in your business, or you've leased a car. You lease a car over a three-year period, for example. At the end of the three-year period the car dealer says, "We're going to give you a great deal. You can buy this car for $15,000." If it's selling on the lot for $20,000, maybe you take it. If the car is available on the lot right now for $8,000, then you say, "Here, catch; I'm going to throw you the keys." You give the investment back to the dealership. That's the beauty of leasing. You can make the decision to buy or give up the lease when the term expires, depending on whether it's a good deal or not.

It's the same idea with LEAPS, isn't it? Why buy the stock if you can lease it? Let's not own the stock and tie up all the money needed to own 100 shares. Let's lease it for up to two-and-a-half years and then have our choice of adding it to our portfolio or turning it back to someone else. I loved that advertising strategy because it explained the LEAPS advantage perfectly. It's too bad they don't use it any more.

LIMITING YOUR RISKS

We're limiting our risk by owning the LEAPS either way. For example, if a stock is trading at $50 and it goes to $51, you've made a dollar. With a LEAPS, you might be able to buy a 50 strike call with 90 days until expiration. Then when the stock goes to $51, your call should go up in value, shouldn't it? (See Table 4.1)

In ballpark figures, what do you think the call will be trading for?

Table 4.1 - **Option Price Behavior**	
Stock Price:	$50→ $51
Days to Expiration:	90 → 90
50 Call:	3 → ?

You bought it at $3. Many investors think, "Well, if the stock is trading at $50 and it goes to $51; the option that was trading for $3 might be trading for $4." That's not the case. If you want an investment that moves point for point with the underlying stock with certainty, you need to buy the stock. Options will not move point for point.

In this particular case, if the stock goes to $51, that option should go from $3 to approximately $3.50. Why did it only go up 50 cents? Well, this tendency is called the delta.

Delta is a measurement of option price change relative to the underlying stock price change. If the stock price changes by $1, then the option price will change by the amount of delta.

If the stock moves a dollar, how is the option expected to perform? In this particular case, the delta was approximately 50 cents. What happens if the stock goes from 51 to 52 the same day? The option that's trading for $3.50 should now be trading for about $4.10. Why? The delta just kicked up a little higher. As the stock price continues in the same direction, the option starts to act more and more like the underlying stock. That's why people buy options.

If I'm correct, then this option should start performing point for point. If our stock is trading at $60, then the option should be worth at least 10 points. If the stock goes to $61, then the call should be worth at least 11 points, plus a little bit of time value premium. The tricky part is that the delta changes. As the stock moves up and down, the delta evolves and changes. As Expiration Friday approaches, delta also changes.

> Computing the trend in delta is a useful tool for timing an exit point, or for seeing how stock volatility affects option valuation.

DELTA AS A FACTOR OF PENDING EXPIRATION

The changing delta is going to be most pronounced as expiration draws near. With expiration two weeks away, the delta of everything on the trading floor will approach either zero (because the option is expiring worthless), or 100, meaning intrinsic value remains and it's going to move exactly or close to the in-the-money price movement of the stock. In this scenario you could say that the option has turned into stock because the in-the-money change mirrors what goes on in that stock.

> When expiration is very close, in-the-money options are expected to mirror changes in stock prices. At this point, the options could be described as having become a form of stock.

Again looking back to past valuation, XYZ was trading at $39 per share. I wanted to buy that 30 strike price call with a 2011 expiration, going out 30 months. The LEAPS option was trading at $14 at that point. What's the delta of this call?

The call gives you the right to buy the stock at $30 while the stock trades at $39. This option is in-the-money by 9 points. I might consider this to be a fairly expensive option. How much is it? (See Table 4.2)

Online Tools

It doesn't hurt to know the delta when you're trading these LEAPS options. The Options Industry Council (OIC) offers free calculation and other tools on their Web site: www.optionseducation.org. For help calculating delta, look for the "Options Investigator" under Trading Tools.

If the stock goes from $39 to $45 in the next 60 days (assuming interest rates and volatility have not changed, and there is still no dividend), this option should go from somewhere around $14 to about $18.70. It would have done fairly well at that point, up $4.70. I would make $4.70 as opposed to $6.00 if I owned the stock instead. But, look at what my investment was. Rather than risking $39 and making $6 (a 15% profit), I risked $14 to make $4.70 (a 33% return). So percentage-wise, I did twice as well owning the LEAPS call.

Table 4.2 - Determining Delta - 30 Call
• XYZ trading at $39
• January 2011 LEAPS 30 call trading at $14
• What is the delta of this call?
If the stock rises from $39 to $45 in 60 days, what will the call price be?

In dollars and cents, I would have done better owning the stock, but two points have to be remembered. First, the percentage return means more because it summarizes the use of money. (For example, I could have bought two calls and made more on a dollars-and-cents basis.) Second, with the option my risks are lower. If this stock had fallen in value, my losses could potentially be huge. But by investing in the option, I can't lose more than the cost of the option, even if the stock plummets.

So there's a trade off. That particular stock only started out with the first dollar move, when it moved from $39 to $40. The option only went up about $0.81 because the delta was in effect. There was not a dollar-for-dollar movement in the option. But as the stock price continues to move in the same direction, and as expiration gets closer, the delta moves higher, approaching 100.

 There's a trade off here. Let Marty help you figure out which is best for you at www.traderslibrary.com/TLEcorner.

Table 4.3 - Determining Delta- 45 Call
• XYZ trading at $39
• January 2011 LEAPS 45 call trading at $7
• What is the delta of this call?
If the stock rises from $39 to $45 in 60 days, what will the call price be?

Consider another example. Instead of buying the 30 call, what if I had bought the 45 strike price LEAPS call? (See Table 4.3) That one was out-of-the-money by 6 points.

What do you think the delta of this call is? The call is out-of-the-money, so the delta will be different than it would be for an in-the-money call.

Delta cannot be applied equally in all situations. When an option is out-of-the-money, delta behaves in a much different manner than with an in-the-money option.

The delta is about 0.52. Remember, we're taking a look at options going out a couple of years. When the stock is at $40, the short-term 40 call and the 40 put have a delta of approximately 0.50. As we go further out in time, the calls pick up a little bit of delta. In this particular case, going out 30 months, the out-of-the-money call has a delta of about 0.52. If the stock rises from $39 to $45, our $7 option goes up to about $9.80.

So the profit is $2.80. Compared to owning the stock, the percentage return is better and the dollar return is worse. With the option,

I risked $7 and we made $2.80, a return of 40%. With the stock, I would have risked $39 to make $6, a return of 15%. I know which one I would prefer.

> With options, the percentage of return is going to be higher than with buying stock because the investment level is much lower.

THE IMPORTANCE OF SETTING TARGETS

When I talk to people about options, I sometimes hear "Hey Marty, I bought this option at $7." I ask, "Where is it going?" They respond, "I don't know." I then ask, "Which expiration month did you buy and when is it going to get to your target?" Some reply that they aren't sure, because they haven't set a target. Most people aren't sure because they haven't set a target. Well, guess what, Houston, we have a problem. You can't trade LEAPS without that target like you can with stocks. *You have to have a target.*

I like to tell people that they have to manage targets sensibly. For example, let's say you're buying an option at $7 and your target is $10. If it gets to $10, then you don't sell as you originally planned; you reexamine it. How do you feel about the option now? If you think it's going to $12, you don't sell. If it does get to $12, you reexamine it again. Perhaps now you think it's going to $15. You know what? You never had a target. Your target was $10, then it was $15, then it became something even higher, perhaps $18. You kept moving the goal line, didn't you?

> If you don't set targets, you have no means for deciding when to close a position. This will certainly increase your chance for losses.

When you trade this way, you've got a problem. It is so important to have a target. Of course, you're allowed to change it, but my point is that you should only change it once, if at all. For example, you're buying an option because you think the stock's going from $39 to $45. You have to have two things: a time limit and a profit target. If you're buying a two-year option, know when you plan to exit the position.

Let's say you purchased 10 of the $7 LEAPS call options on a stock that did well, and the options are now trading at $15. You feel the stock still has potential to move higher, but you're getting a little nervous. Here's a question: if you didn't own these options, would you buy them at $15? You could sell half of the position, or you could trade them in for a higher strike call and pocket the difference, a credit to you. You could sell some out-of-the-money, shorter-term calls, turning the position into a time-diagonal spread. In other words, it is not an all-or-nothing situation; there could be many strategies in between.

Options decay, so before your option really starts to fall off the table in terms of value, you should hand it off to someone else. So you need either a target on the option, or a target on the stock. Remember, if your target doesn't work by a certain date, you should do something—sell or reevaluate.

> These three important tools will help you reduce losses and know when it is time to exit: profit target, time target, and stop-loss.

Once you have a profit target and a time target, you might find that either the movement in the stock or the movement in the option just isn't working. We should probably go back to point number one on our analysis here. "Why did I pick this stock? This isn't working." If it isn't working, get out.

The nice thing about LEAPS is we're giving ourselves a lot of time. We don't have to panic. If the option goes from $7 to $5.50 two weeks from now, we've still got two years to make this thing work. But there should be a point in time with any investment where, if it isn't working, you sell and cut your losses. In this case, you can do the same thing with LEAPS that you would do with stocks.

Have the discipline to exit the trade. That's the toughest thing a professional trader ever has to do: take a loss. I can still remember the first big loss I took. Believe it or not, it was like the weight of the world was off my shoulders. I could step back and reexamine it. I later reentered the same position at a lower price and made money.

Granted, it is tough to take a loss. But then you can step back and look at it analytically. A good way to set up the contingency is with a stop-loss order. A stop-loss order is used by traders and investors to exit a position if the underlying starts to move the wrong way. For example, you buy an option for $5. You could enter a stop-loss order at $4, meaning if the option goes down to $4, then enter a market order to sell—get me out! There are variations on this, like a "trailing stop." In this example, the option you bought at $5 went up to $9, but you have a trailing stop order $1 below. As the option moved higher, you always had a stop order $1 below the highest price. With the option at $9, the stop would be at $8, if it went to $9.30 the stop would be at $8.30. If any of your target points fail and the value declines, the stop-loss gets you out.

One word of warning about stop-losses: I have seen some investors set very "tight" stops. For example, buying an option at $5.00 and entering a stop order at $4.25, only $0.75 below the option purchase price. This stop order could be triggered with a $1.00 move in the underlying. Brokerage firms handle stop orders differently, so find out how your broker would handle your stop-order. These three important exit points are summarized in Table 4.4.

Table 4.4 - Important Exit Points	
	• Profit target
Have three exit points in mind:	• Time limit
	• Stop-loss point
Have the discipline to exit the trade when any of the points is reached.	

PROS AND CONS SUMMARY

Pros

Trading LEAPS versus trading stock offers you distinct advantages. The required investment amount is lower, so you leverage your capital. Risk is also lower because you cannot lose more than the limited amount you invest. Even though that is potentially 100%, the dollars at risk are less than when buying stock. You also may get a much higher percentage of profit when the option works out profitably, compared to the returns on stock.

Cons

The disadvantages include larger percentage losses with options. You can lose 100% if the option value goes to zero and you don't take any action. That's less likely with stock, where you can cut your

Table 4.5 - Trading LEAPS vs. Trading Stock	
LEAPS Advantages	• Lower investment
	• Lower risk
	• Potentially higher percentage profit
LEAPS Disadvantages	• Lower absolute profit
	• Potentially larger percentage loss
	• No dividends, voting rights

losses after a decline, or simply wait out the market until the price level returns. Also, with options you receive no dividends. With LEAPS trading, you have the right to own the underlying stock, but because you don't own it, you don't get the dividend if there is one. You don't get the voting rights. You don't get invited to the annual meeting. (So you miss out on the IBM meeting in Armonk, New York, where I hear the box lunch is catered by United Airlines. It's supposed to be very, very good!)

You don't have any of the rights of owning a stock. You can exercise your option at any point in time with a LEAPS option, but you don't have the same rights as stockholders when you don't own the stock. The pros and cons of LEAPS call options versus stocks are summarized in Table 4.5.

SELF-TEST QUESTIONS

1. Buying LEAPS is like leasing a car because:

    a. you have to turn it in after three years.

    b. upkeep is your responsibility.

    c. you have the right, but not the obligation, to convert to a purchase.

    d. it always ends up costing less in any situation.

2. The option's delta is a measurement of:

    a. option price change in relation to the underlying stock's price change.

    b. point cost per time increment.

    c. the number of points the option is in-the-money as a percentage of the price per share of the underlying stock.

    d. the rate of decline in time value.

3. Delta tends to increase when:

    a. the option moves out-of-the-money and at least 12 months remain until expiration.

    b. the option moves further in-the-money and expiration gets closer.

    c. stock price volatility declines and downside volume exceeds upside volume.

    d. you buy multiple option contracts and stock price remains in a very narrow trading range.

4. Advantages of buying LEAPS instead of stock include:

    a. higher percentage profit possible.

    b. lower initial cost.

    c. lower market risk.

    d. all of the above.

5. Disadvantages of buying LEAPS instead of stock include:

    a. always lower percentage profit.

    b. no dividends or voting rights.

    c. higher initial cost.

    d. all of the above.

For answers, go to www.traderslibrary.com/TLEcorner.

Chapter 5

COVERED WRITING WITH LEAPS

The covered writing of LEAPS is an interesting alternative strategy to the more traditional covered call on stock. Why not use the LEAPS as a stock substitute? You are probably familiar with the basic covered call (if not, please refer to the glossary), but I want to explain how you can use LEAPS in a *time-diagonal spread*.

COVERED WRITE STRATEGY

This strategy is popular because of its safe, conservative use of options. To use this strategy, you must own 100 shares of the underlying stock. Sell a call against those shares, and you receive the premium. If the call is exercised, your 100 shares are called away at the strike price. To avoid exercise, you can close the position by buying the call, or you can roll it out in time, exchanging the short call for one that expires later. The new short call could be the same strike price. You may see or hear the latter referred to as rolling up and out—up to a higher call strike price if more bullish, and out in time to a later dated expiration. A variation on this idea is to substitute a long LEAPS call for stock and then write short-term calls against it. Table 5.1 summarizes the components of this strategy for a stock I am calling XYZ, valued at $49.

Table 5.1 · Covered Writing with LEAPS
Using LEAPS as a stock substitute to create a position similar to a covered write (known as a time-diagonal spread).
Example:
XYZ @ $49.00 on 11/01/08
Buy 1 XYZ Jan 2010 40 call @ $14.00
Sell 1 XYZ Dec 2008 55 call @ $1.65

A traditional stockholder approach would be to simply buy 100 shares of XYZ at $49 per share, putting out $4,900 plus trading costs. But, instead, I can enter the spread shown in Table 5.1. It involves buying one XYZ January call going out almost 15 months. I choose the 40 strike price, which costs $14 ($1,400). At the same time, I sell a short-term option; this creates the spread. (A long and a short option on the same stock is a spread.) In this example, I select a call expiring in about 45 days that is 6 points out-of-the-money, with a strike of 55.

So my net cost is $1,235 (14 points for the long LEAPS minus 1.65 points for the short call). This is about one-fourth of the cost of simply buying 100 shares. I substitute the LEAPS for the stock, which reminds us why the LEAPS is defined as a security. It replaces the long stock position but gives me control over the same 100 shares.

> You can create a covered call using a LEAPS option in place of stock, which costs less and reduces your risk.

Remember, these examples do not include trading costs; you have to calculate the cost of buying and selling. Also, you usually have to have a margin account set up for covered call writing, so you first have to make sure your broker enables this type of trade. You also have to be pre-approved to trade options in spread positions. Finally, some firms allow trades like this in retirement accounts, some do not. Therefore, if you're planning to trade these strategies in your IRA or other tax-deferred account, check your brokerage firm's policies beforehand.

EVOLVING VALUE SCENARIOS

Now let's take a look at how these values are likely to evolve. Table 5.2 provides the first scenario.

In this instance, after 45 days, we assume the stock remains unchanged at $49 per share. The December 55 call that was trading for $1.65 is now worth zero, so we're up $1.65 on the overall trade.

Table 5.2 - Covered Writing with LEAPS - Scenario 1
At December '08 option expiration
Stock price: $49.00 (unchanged)   Dec. '08 55 call: $1.65 → 0 + $1.65   Jan '10 40 call: $14.00 → ?
If short-term call expires, do it again

The important thing for me is how my long LEAPS call performs. I purchased it for $14 but since then it would have had some time decay. I estimate that 45 days of time decay in this case brings that option down roughly $0.50 cents. So I cannot just collect that $1.65 profit from the short call as if it was free money. I still have to live with the risk that the stock could move lower. Even when the stock remains at the same price, I have some time decay. But remember, this 40 LEAPS call is my stock surrogate. I've invested a net of $1,235 rather than $4,900, and that is a tremendous advantage. So comparing the profit on the short call versus time decay before transaction costs, I'm up about $1.15. ($1.65 for the short call minus $0.50 cents for time decay.)

If the short-term call expires, I can simply repeat the process. Selling options was the first strategy I got involved with years ago, when I discovered the pleasures and profits in writing covered calls. In my case, I owned some shares of stock in the company I worked for at the time. To me it was a lot—well, it was all my money. I had about 1,500 shares of the stock. I would sell 4 or 5 call options against it. The idea was something close to this strategy, focusing on selling out-of-the-money positions like this.

> You have an advantage in writing shorter-term short calls. They will expire worthless as long as they remain out-of-the-money. That means the option position can be all profit.

It makes sense to use this approach. If the stock goes above the strike price chosen for the covered write, I would be assigned and perhaps diversify into a different position. If it doesn't get to that level, selling 5 of these options for $1.65 brings in $825. That's a nice "dividend" to collect.

So, yes, I can write another short call and, in fact, as long as these keep expiring, I can replace them indefinitely. That is one of the great advantages to the strategy; it is safe because you own the stock. In the event you are assigned, you decided on the call strike price you sold, so you will make so you will make a profit on the option, the stock, and from dividends—a triple win. If they expire worthless, you go right back in and do it again.

> There is no limit to how many times you can sell covered calls. Once they expire, you can open another and repeat the process as many times as you wish.

When the Stock's Price Rises

Now let's look at a second scenario. What happens if the stock's price goes up significantly? Table 5.3 shows what occurs in this instance.

Table 5.3 - Covered Writing with LEAPS - Scenario 2
At December '08 option expiration
Stock price: $59.00 (stock up big, $10) Dec. '08 55 call: $1.65 → 4.00 - $2.35 Jan '10 40 call: $14.00 → ?
Short-term call is ITM! Assigned?

I'm using the example of the stock rising to $59 per share. Now remember, I previously sold the 55 strike, and since then, the stock rallied 10 points. The call I sold for $1.65 has risen to $4. If I were to close this out, I'd be down $2.35 on the short 55 strike call. Meanwhile, the LEAPS call I bought at $14 has gone up to about $21.75. So, I am up by $7.75 on my long position. On a net basis, I'm still up $5.40 ($7.75 minus $2.35).

The short call is in-the-money. What happens if it is assigned? There are different approaches that I can use. First, I can buy stock and deliver it at the strike. Or as an alternative, I can exercise my long LEAPS call. But in this example, it would not make sense for me to exercise the LEAPS call. With the stock at $59, the 40 call is 19 points in-the-money. But it is trading at $21.75, so there is still $2.75 of time value premium remaining.

Remember, your net position is calculated by subtracting short profit/ loss from long profit/loss. When the stock price rises, you have a favorable range of choices.

Remember that option premium consists of two elements—time value and intrinsic value. I can certainly exercise the LEAPS and deliver the shares to answer the assignment. But by doing that, I'd be throwing away my 2.75 points of time value, which is $275. I would rather keep my $275.

> The difference between time value and intrinsic value defines profitability in the spread; so your analysis has to include a critical view of changed option values.

If the intention is to exit this position completely, as an alternative to exercising the LEAPS, sell the LEAPS for $21.75 and buy 100 shares at $59, closing both open positions. The time premium of $2.75 would be retained, and you would have no position in the stock, LEAPS or option.

You can do it either way. Remember, assignment is almost always certain when the short call is in-the-money at expiration, but an early assignment most likely occurs either in the last few days before expiration, or if the stock is about to pay a dividend. There is always a chance the stock price will retreat enough so the short call goes out-of-the-money, but in this case, I'm assuming exercise is inevitable; it forces my decision. Roll the short position, close the entire position, or accept the probable assignment and deal with it after expiration.

With exercise, the picture is interesting. Even though my position was assigned last night by the Options Clearing Corporation, I got the notice today from my broker. If I exercise the LEAPS call, I'm actually exercising it one day late. That's allowable. If I buy stock and sell the LEAPS call, I have to put up margin for one day. But if I'm going to pocket $275, I can put up the margin for one day. That's okay with me. It's a point worth considering, especially if you take this strategy up into multiples involving many more positions and much more money.

When the Stock's Price Falls

A third scenario is what happens when the stock price falls. Table 5.4 illustrates the situation when the stock falls from $49 down to $39.

In this situation, the short 55 call certainly expires worthless; but the LEAPS option I'm holding in a long position has fallen from $14 down to approximately $6.65. That's a loss of $7.35 on the investment. Even subtracting the profit on the short call of the entire $1.65, I'm still down $5.70.

Table 5.4 - Covered Writing with LEAPS - Scenario 3
At December '08 option expiration
Stock price: $39.00 (stock down big, $10) Dec '08 55 call: 1.65 → 0 + 1.65 Jan '10 40 call: 14.00 → ?
Stock price decline - stop-loss point?

Do The Math

Original purchase price of LEAPS	$1,400
Less current value	- 665
Loss	$ 735
Profit on expired short call	- 165
Net loss	$ 570

This is not as dire as it seems. The current loss of $570 has to be compared to what would have happened if I had bought 100 shares of stock. I'd be down 10 points. In comparison, this position is only down $570, a difference of $430.

Now I can strategize the position in a new way. I am still free to sell covered calls, but I have to remember that my original position was based on the stock's value at $49. So if I sell a call with a strike price too low and the stock rises, I might not participate as much as I wanted to. I am covered on the short call option with my long 40 LEAPS strike, but of course I would prefer that the stock rise a few points before re-entering the spread with another short call. I still own the long 40 LEAPS, so I can wait out the price, hoping it will rise. If and when it does, I can revert to my original strategy, but right now I might have to wait out the position loss of $570.

 You might be wondering, "why buy the 40 strike price?" and not some other strike? Marty explains at www.traderslibrary.com/TLEcorner.

Early in this chapter, we discussed rolling an option position up-and-out as a stock rises, so could we roll an option down-and-out if the stock falls? Sure. With XYZ falling from $49 to $39, an alternative could be to buy back the short December 55 call at $0.05, and sell a January ('09) 45 strike call, and collect roughly $1.50. The 45 strike is over 15% out-of-the-money with 4-5 weeks until January expiration. Ideally, XYZ moves higher but stays below $45, so the short option expires worthless.

> Even when your spread position shows a loss because stock value has fallen, it will not be as severe as the loss you would have experienced in buying 100 shares of stock.

Remember, this example was based on buying a January 40 LEAPS call option. You might be wondering why I picked the 40 strike call. In this case, I wanted a LEAPS that mimicked stock ownership to the greatest degree possible. By purchasing an in-the-money LEAPS option, I achieved this. This particular option had a negative delta of 81. In comparison, a call 6 points out-of-the-money only had a negative delta of 15 or 20. If I thought the stock would creep up a bit higher, that short-term option would be swimming upstream, while the in-the-money option would have mirrored the price and action of the stock.

> The key to success in this spread is the delta; this is why you want your long LEAPS to be in-the-money and your short call to be out-of-the-money.

Even so, why did I pick the 40 and not a different strike price? There may not be a 45 strike LEAPS available. The 50 LEAPS option would be out-of-the-money and all-time premium, which defeats this delta advantage. I picked the 40 because I wanted to mimic stock movement. Again, that meant I had to buy an in-the-money option.

THE LONG-TERM ADVANTAGE

What happens if the stock drops down and I become bearish on that stock? Let's say that I initiated this position and the stock then went from $49 to $39. Am I still bullish? If I am, then I hold on to that LEAPS option and wait out the price. Remember, I still have over one year to go until the LEAPS expires. If I become bearish, the best strategy is… sell the LEAPS call; exit the position!

The point is, if I still like the investment, I want to continue to write options against it. If I move down my strike price, I'm also moving down my break even point by bringing in premium. I'm also limiting my potential upside, but only for a short term.

Be careful when you bring your break even point down. It could result in a more likely assignment and reduced profits on the overall position.

When the stock goes down, you have the covered write, and if you still like the stock, you continue to write against it. You roll down the short call; go down and out. In other words, covered calls are very flexible strategies and allow you to take all kinds of positions.

Table 5.5 - Important Strategy Features	
Potential profit	= $6.00 in 50 days (11/1–12/19)
Initial investment	= 12.35 (14.00 – 1.65)
Percentage profit	= 48% in 50 days
• Risk limited to initial investment + commission	
• Risk of early assignment on short call	
• Profit potential and percentage profit are estimates only, assuming XYZ at $55 or higher.	
• Usually done in a margin account.	
• All examples do not include commissions and are not intended to be recommendations.	

Every time you make a profit on the covered call, you reduce your exposure and your break even.

The risk, though, in taking those covered positions too low is that eventually the stock will rebound (we hope) and you'll be exercised. The spread differential between your long LEAPS strike and your short covered call could represent a net loss, so you have to be sure you know where your break even lies.

The beauty of this strategy, overall, is that it offers lower risk when the stock price falls. I'm not risking $49 per share as I would by buying the stock; I'm risking $14 by buying the LEAPS option that will mimic the stock's price.

Not only can you leverage your capital with the LEAPS spread, you can also reduce risk if and when the stock's price falls.

IMPORTANT FEATURES OF THE STRATEGY

To summarize this strategy, look at the features: initial investment, timing, and profit. Take a look at Table 5.5.

The profit potential with the stock was $6 in 50 days. With the initial net investment of $1,235, that's about a 50% return in less than two months. If you annualize this, it is pretty fantastic. No one in a brokerage firm is allowed to annualize profits on positions under two months, and it should only count for comparisons anyway. So if you have two different positions with the same dollar profit but different holding periods, annualizing the returns keeps things in perspective. That's the benefit. You can't annualize a 50-day return and then expect to duplicate that all year.

In this example, your risk would be limited to your original net investment, adjusted by trading costs. In comparison, when you buy 100 shares of stock, you put out more cash and you have more risk. However, you also face the risk of early exercise with the short side of the spread, if and when it goes in-the-money. It's an acceptable risk, however, because you have the choice of using the long LEAPS to satisfy assignment.

 Are you at greater risk buying deeper in-the-money calls? Find out at www.traderslibrary.com/TLEcorner.

Strategies based on being assigned the short call are:

- Re-purchase the stock and sell another short-term call—reinitiate the LEAPS covered call position.
- Re-purchase the stock and stay long the LEAPS call—the net position is long a LEAPS call.
- Close the entire position by purchasing stock and selling the LEAPS call.
- Close the position by exercising a LEAPS call (not advised if there is time premium in the LEAPS call).

First, you can simply purchase shares of stock and satisfy assignment, and then duplicate the original spread by selling another short call. Second, you can purchase stock to satisfy the call and continue holding the long LEAPS. Third, you can close the entire position by purchasing stock and selling your LEAPS. Fourth, you can close the position by exercising the LEAPS; however, this means you are giving up any remaining time value premium.

The questions you have to ask if the stock price declines are:

- Will you sell the LEAPS call at a loss?
- Will you write another short-term call with a lower strike price?
- Will you keep the LEAPS call without selling another short-term call against it?

In conclusion, the covered call strategy, which combines the owning of a long LEAPS call and selling a short-term call option, gives you a lot of flexibility. Because delta in the two option positions is vastly different when the in-the-money and out-of-the-money re-lationship is far apart, you get a beneficial squeeze in price changes as the stock moves higher. Whether stock price rises or falls, you have a lot of choices. As long as you pick the one that produces the most advantageous outcome based on your outlook, you can profit from the strategy of covering the LEAPS in place of the more traditional covering of the stock.

In any strategy, identify the range of risks and then decide which are accept-able and which are not. That will define the strategies you should use.

SELF-TEST QUESTIONS

1. When you write covered calls on LEAPS long positions instead of the underlying stock:

   a. it creates a bull straddle.

   b. the LEAPS option acts as a stock substitute.

   c. you must own 100 shares of the underlying stock.

   d. all of the above.

2. A time-diagonal spread involves:

   a. a long LEAPS expiring further out in time than a short call.

   b. a short LEAPS expiring further out in time than a long call.

   c. a long and short call with identical expiration dates.

   d. two very short-term options, a call and a put.

3. The covered LEAPS strategy relies on:

   a. differences in the delta of an out-of-the-money long LEAPS and an in-the-money short call.

   b. identical delta in both long and short positions.

   c. a zero delta in the short call, essential to avoid assignment.

   d. differences in the delta of an in-the-money long LEAPS and an out-of-the-money short call.

4. If a short call opened in a time-diagonal spread expires:

    a. you can open another one, repeating the same step indefinitely until the long position expires.

    b. the long LEAPS must be exercised immediately.

    c. you will be required to buy 100 shares of the underlying stock.

    d. the entire position ends up as a net loss.

5. If the short call in the time-diagonal spread goes in-the-money, and is assigned, you can:

    a. buy stock and deliver it at the strike.

    b. exercise the long LEAPS to satisfy assignment.

    c. close out both sides of the position.

    d. any of the above.

For answers, go to www.traderslibrary.com/TLEcorner.

Chapter 6

LEAPS PROTECTIVE PUTS AND COLLARS

Let's say you want the benefit of stock ownership (dividends, voting rights, etc.) but you have concerns about price depreciation in the future. Here's an intriguing idea for you to consider: the married put. The married put is created when you buy stock and a put at the same time in order to protect against depreciation in the stock's price. Basically, you are buying an insurance policy on the value of that stock (assuming you own 100 shares for each put you buy).

> The married put limits downside risk while leaving upside potential in place.

With a LEAPS put, you overcome a problem that occurs when using short-term options. The LEAPS put provides long-term insurance—as much as two-and-a-half years. This certainly limits the market risk of the long stock position during the life of the put. At the same time, you still have unlimited profit potential. I have never owned an investment that went to unlimited, but theoretically it's possible. With the married put, you own stock with uncapped upside potential. In comparison to covered calls, you limit your growth because the short call can be exercised and your stock called away.

 For a specific example featuring Home Depot stock, check out www.traderslibrary.com/TLEcorner.

For example, let's say you bought 100 shares of a stock 1 month ago when it was trading at $30. Looking ahead about 18 months, you could buy a 30 put for about $5.25. What's your risk? The bottom-line risk is $5.25 no matter how low the stock goes. If share value goes to $10, you have the right to sell that stock at $30 per share because you own the put. For each point the stock falls, the in-the-money put will rise one point in intrinsic value. The risk is limited to the premium paid. That premium will vary based on the difference between current market value and strike price. For example, if the stock were at $31 and you bought the $30 put, you would be $1 out-of-the-money. Your risk would be $5.25 plus the $1 deductible.

When you reduce downside risk to a percentage compared to unlimited upside, you can appreciate the strategic advantage of the married put.

FIGURE 6.1- LEAPS - Married Puts.

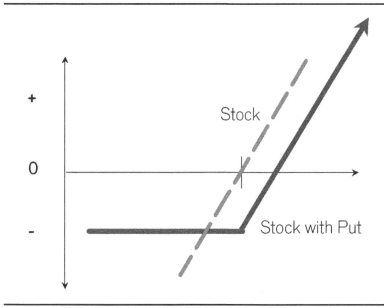

If the stock were trading at $29, that option would be in-the-money by 1 point. Your risk would only be $4.25. The example I give is at-the-money because the math is pretty simple when trading exactly at the strike. So, in this example, you have about 17.5% risk for 18 months ($5.25 ÷ $30)—but your profit potential is unlimited.

 When considering a married put trade, you should consider the diversity of your portfolio. To find out why, watch the online video at www.traderslibrary.com.TLEcorner.

Those who understand option terminology will realize that a married put is the equivalent of a synthetic call. Figure 6.1 shows the outcome of owning stock compared to the outcome of owning stock with a long put. The downside is protected because losses in the stock are offset by gains in the put. The upside profit potential, though, is unlimited.

THE INEVITABLE TAX COMPLICATION

There are different tax reasons to use the married put.

The concept of the LEAPS married put is sound, but there are two reasons why more investors do not use it.

First, there is a commission cost involved. If you buy stock and buy a LEAPS married put, there are two commissions to pay. Second, the tax situation is complex, and you might not be able to deduct a loss in the year it happens with the married put. You will probably have to treat both sides of the transaction as two sides of the same strategy, so tax rules are inhibiting.

Taxes & Investing

For comprehensive information on option taxes, contact any one of the exchanges for a FREE copy of the booklet *Taxes and Investing: A Guide for the Individual Investor*. You can also download it at http://www.cboe.com/LearnCenter/pdf/TaxesandInvesting.pdf or call The Options Industry Council at 1-888-OPTIONS. It covers almost every scenario you can think of as to how taxes work on various option strategies.

The investor who will be attracted to the married put position will be thinking about how the market is going to perform. If the market and the economy do well, the stock starts to perform to the upside. At that point, when the market risk has passed, the investor with a married put asks, "Why don't I sell that put option and get what I can for it? I still own the stock. I no longer need the insurance."

A married put implies that you're buying stock and buying a put on the same day, but you don't necessarily have to. You can cover the long stock position with a put if you're worried about volatility.

You don't have to enter both sides of a married put at the same time. The position can also be created in phases.

THE PROTECTIVE PUT

A LEAPS protective put is another interesting variation. The attributes of this strategy are summarized in Table 6.1.

In this case, you already own shares and you're concerned about the economy, interest rates, the election, the Euro dollar—whatever

Table 6.1 - LEAPS Protective Puts
• Already own shares
• Concerned about ? ? ? ?
• Don't wish to sell shares now
• Tax considerations?
• Buy LEAPS puts as "term insurance"

scares you. But you don't want to sell your shares. So you buy a put as a type of term insurance.

In a strategy like this, you have to be aware of the tax considerations. Buying protective LEAPS puts can arrest the holding period on stock if you've had it less than 12 months. That means that if you sell, you might not get those long-term capital gains you were counting on.

> Consider the tax consequences of the protective put. It may convert a long-term capital gain to a short-term gain.

A number of put strategies can help even with the tax ramifications. If you're buying in-the-money puts, the capital gains holding period may be set back to zero. So be sure you're careful and that you know what is going to happen with your taxes. The free publication *Taxes and Investing: A Guide for the Individual Investor* explains all of these issues in common sense terms, so I encourage everyone to get it from the Options Industry Council and read it carefully.

PROS AND CONS OF LEAPS PUTS

You should always study the pros and cons of any strategy before you jump into it. (See Table 6.2)

Pros

The primary pros of LEAPS puts are (1) protection at a fixed cost for a relatively long period of time, which eliminates much of the risk; (2) flexibility; and (3) limited cost for limited risk.

Cons

On the downside, this kind of protection can also be expensive. It increases your overall cost, making your break even point higher; and puts will expire in the future.

In the last example, your insurance cost 17.5% of your investment value. This increase in your cost also means your break even point is going to be higher. Remember, the LEAPS put is going to expire in the future, but your stock will not expire. So that downside risk will eventually come back. A periodic check is important, just so

Table 6.2 - LEAPS Puts - Pros & Cons	
Pros	• Protection at a fixed cost
	• Flexibility: keep shares and dividends
	• Limited cost / limited risk
Cons	• Protection can be expensive
	• Increases overall cost / break even
	• Puts expire, stock does not
	• Periodic check is essential

you keep perspective. You can't eliminate risk, but you can reduce it for a period of time.

Going back to the example of owning 100 shares of stock at $30 and buying a put with a 30 strike: consider what you will need to do if, for example, 7 months later the stock is trading at $40 per share. You still have your protective put. But with the put's strike at 30, you now have a 10-point risk, from $40 per share down to $30 per share. If you think of this point spread as a deductible on your insurance, you might decide at this point that the 30 put is the wrong insurance policy.

> Think of the option premium as an insurance cost to eliminate risk for the time between purchase and expiration.

The periodic check-up of a protective put may require you to re-think the strategy based on how the stock price has changed. Are you still worried? Should you move the insurance up to a different strike price? Perhaps buy a 35 strike put or 37.50 put if available, and sell the long 30 put. This would be "rolling up" your put protection for a small debit.

THE COLLAR STRATEGY

The collar strategy is actually very simple. In a collar, you own stock, and you sell a call option against it, then you use the proceeds to buy a protective put. For example, in a traditional collar you own

100 shares of the underlying stock and create a collar when you sell an out-of-the-money call and buy an out-of-the money put.

> The collar has three elements: long stock, covered short call, and a long protective put.

Let's look at an example. You own 100 shares of stock at $75 per share. You buy a 70 put with the proceeds from selling a 90 call. This provides you with an interesting form of protection.

You gain the right to sell 100 shares at 70 from the long put. You have an obligation to deliver 100 shares at 90 if called upon to do so. The call premium reduces the cost of the put. You may hear this referred to as a zero cost collar. Some options terms are used interchangeably, which, of course, confuses things. Zero cost is as it sounds. The money you bring in offsets the cost of the insurance policy that you buy.

You can collar all or part of a large holding with the LEAPS option. When low-cost protection is desirable, this is a viable solution. Now, this is where it gets interesting. Let me give you an example: looking back a few years when I came up with this, I often said that I planned to retire in late 2008. Like many people, I simply update my estimated retirement date every year or two, rolling it forward like a short option.

> The collar is a valuable strategy for large holdings and for retirement planning.

In this example, my retirement had been set for late 2008. I owned $750,000 of XYZ. Based on my target retirement date, I knew I couldn't retire on less than $600,000. I would like to hold on to the stock for a while, but I don't want to wake up one day to find out the stock is trading at $400,000 or less. But even though I want the upside profit, I can't afford to buy puts. This scenario is summarized in Table 6.3.

Table 6.3 - LEAPS Collar Case Study
• You plan to retire in late 2008.
• You own $750,000 of XYZ.
• You cannot afford to let the value fall below $600,000.
• You want some upside.
• You can't afford to buy puts.

What can I do? I would like to buy some protective puts, but they are too expensive. There is a solution. I own 10,000 shares of XYZ trading at 75. Why not buy 87 of the January '09 70 strike price puts? That's 5 points out-of-the-money, but if I pay $13 for these, that's an expensive option!

One solution is to sell 90 of the January '09 90 strike price calls. That's 15 points out-of-the-money and I would collect $11.60. But I'm only protecting 8,700 shares by buying 87 of the 70 strike LEAPS puts. My net cost for 87 of these collars is $1.40 a piece ($12,180) because I'm spending $13 and I'm bringing in $11.60.

By selling those 3 additional call options on the stock I own, I'm bringing in another $3,480. So my net cost is $8,700. To protect my portfolio of $750,000, I'm spending $8,700. For these calculations, I suggest using a worksheet like the one shown in Table 6.4.

Again looking back to when this plan was devised, what happens on Expiration Friday in January 2009? Let's say the stock gets clobbered and is trading at $40 per share. I have the right to sell 8,700 shares at $70. That's $609,000 (and I still own 1,300 shares worth an additional $52,000). I've had a little bit of commission, but I'm still up over $600,000. That was one of my main goals, remember, to protect $600,000 of the $750,000. If the stock is above 90, I have to deliver 9,000 shares at $90. That's $810,000, less my commission. I started out with $750,000. The bonus here is if the stock goes higher than $90, I still own 1,000 shares. I protected 8,700 shares.

Table 6.4 - LEAPS Collar Case Study - Worksheet
Own 10,000 shares XYZ at 75.00
Buy 87 Jan '09 70 puts at 13.00
Sell 90 Jan '09 90 calls at 11.60
Net cost per collar = 1.40
Cost of hedge = 87 x $140
* All examples do not include commissions and are not intended to be recommendations.

If the stock is above 90, I still own 1,000 shares, so I haven't capped off my upside. I just put on my insurance policy. I wanted to maintain a minimum of $600,000; I currently have $810,000 plus at least 1,000 shares trading over $90.

If nothing happens, that is, if the stock doesn't move, I still have $750,000 less that amount to initiate the trade. Does this strategy match up with your outlook on the shares, or your concern about protecting the majority of the capital in those shares? Would you be happy to sell most of the shares (9,000) at $90? If so, this could be the absolute best strategy to use. This shows where you can flip back and forth. You don't have to cover 100% of everything. You don't have to do everything on a one-to-one basis. You can

Table 6.5 - Using a LEAPS Collar - Option 2
Buy 100 shares of XYZ at $ 75.00
Buy 1 XYZ Jan '09 70 put 13.00
Sell 1 XYZ Jan '09 90 call 11.60
Net Cost: $76.40
Risk: $ 6.40 (8.5%)
Potential Gain: $13.60 (17.8%)
above example excludes transaction costs

FIGURE 6.2 - LEAPS Collar Option 2 - Outcome

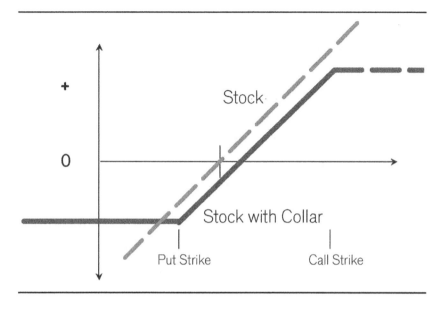

be as flexible as you want. Figure 6.2 shows the collar strategy and its outcome.

You might wonder how the delta works out on the overall position. You could observe that the delta is a little less than 50% on the puts and 100% on your stock. But in this case, I would not be particularly concerned about delta. If the stock moves lower, the negative delta on the protective puts increases, while the positive delta of the calls you sold decreases. Below $70 per share, the delta on Expiration Friday is 100 on the 87 puts you own. That's the concern. In the example, I offset 8% risk to the downside with 18% or more potential gain.

PUTS AS TRAINING WHEELS ON YOUR PORTFOLIO

I know a broker out in California who likes to initiate trades like this. He used to say, "I think we should be involved in XYZ." I'd reply, "I'm not going to get involved in anything. I hate the market." So he'd come back saying, "I think you should diversify into that sector and I think XYZ is the best of breed. Our firm loves XYZ and has a 12-18 month price target 15% - 20% higher."

"Why don't we put this on as a package? Why don't we buy a stock with training wheels?" And he was right. The most you can lose in this example is roughly 8%; yet, you can make 18% or more. Plus, you're entitled to any dividends in the stock through the whole period.

> Like many option positions, puts work best as a package that includes cost reduction.

So you don't have to necessarily limit your choices because puts are expensive. This example presents a case where you could initiate the position as a package.

There's no monopoly on good ideas. Owning 10,000 shares and buying 87 puts and selling 90 calls lets you mix and match all you want. You can also mix and match expirations. You can buy the 15-month LEAPS put and sell a 9-month regular call option.

There's no magic in which strike price and which month you put into action. The beauty of options—remembering the time advantages with LEAPS—is that you have a very wide range of potential.

> Time erosion on short-term options can be severe—always a problem for the long option position. Time erosion for LEAPS, however, is a small element.

By remembering how time decay works, owning a LEAPS option gives you a clear advantage over owning a traditional option. Time usually works against you, but holding a long position long-term exposes you to more growth potential. This observation also applies when you are selling options.

For example, if you sell an 18-month LEAPS call, you might bring in $1,000 or so. If the stock or index goes nowhere, a month from now that option may be trading for about the same or only a little less. You would have sold an expensive option, but the time decay may be negligible for quite a while.

PROS AND CONS OF LEAPS COLLARS

Let's take a look at the pros and cons of LEAPS collars. As with all strategies, there are always good and bad aspects. (See Table 6.6)

Primarily, you get protection at a reduced cost (to purchasing a put) in purchasing a collar. The risk/reward ratio is favorable as well. On the con side, the strategy limits your upside potential due to the short call strike and the long time period. As a final negative, you have to also consider the possibility of early exercise. Any time the short position is in-the-money, it can be exercised. It's a small risk, but you have to plan for it and decide in advance that you'll still be happy if the stock is called away before you'd like.

Table 6.6 - **LEAPS Collars - Pros and Cons**	
Pros	• Protection at a reduced cost
	• Favorable risk/reward ratio
Cons	• Limited upside
	• Limited time period
	• If stock sharply higher, adjust strike

SELF-TEST QUESTIONS

1. A married put is created when:

    a. you sell a put against shorted stock.

    b. you buy a put and you short stock.

    c. you buy a put and you buy stock.

    d. you sell a put and you buy stock.

2. The married put is the equivalent of:

    a. a single put.

    b. a married call.

    c. a multiple-ladder put.

    d. a synthetic call.

3. Under federal tax rules, with a married put:

    a. you may not be able to deduct losses until both sides of the transaction have been closed.

    b. you cannot claim any loss deductions.

    c. the tax rate is lower than the rate for a single put.

    d. taxes can be avoided by offsetting the position with an equally costly married call.

4. A protective put is one you buy:

    a. to avoid or defer taxes.

    b. as a form of term insurance.

    c. as an alternative to the married put.

    d. all of the above.

5. One tax consideration with the married put is:

    a. the possibility of losing all your write-offs in the current year.

    b. arrest or re-set the long-term capital gains holding period to day one.

    c. the trigger of the passive loss rule.

    d. all of the above.

For answers, go to www.traderslibrary.com/TLEcorner.

Chapter 7

A YEAR-END LEAPS TAX STRATEGY

My year-end LEAPS tax strategy works well for the scenario presented in Table 7.1.

The scenario is this: you own stock that has gone down in value. You're thinking of selling it for a tax loss before December 31, and you're aware of the wash sale rule.

Table 7.1 - A Year-End LEAPS Tax Strategy	
Consider the "LEAPS Tax Strategy"	
Example:	Bought 100 shares XYZ at $65
Current Price:	$35

> ## The Wash Sale Rule
>
> If you close an investment holding before December 31, you can claim the loss unless you re-open it within 30 days or if you establish a like position 30 days before or after the sale. If you do, it is treated as a wash sale and the deduction cannot be taken.

You can sell the stock in the last week of December and write off the loss, planning to repurchase in the first week of February at least 31 days later. By doing that, however, you're out of the market for 30 days or more. Depreciated stock can be used to reduce taxes, but you have to also be aware of the timing for repurchase if you want the loss to count.

THE THANKSGIVING-CHRISTMAS-SUPER BOWL SPREAD

There is another way to claim year-end losses. How about buying an additional 100 shares of the same stock in November and then selling the original shares before December 31, at least 31 days later? By doing this, you are allowed to claim the loss (on the original 100 shares) but you still own the stock.

> The wash sale rule applies for 30 days both before and after a sale, so you have to plan ahead and time your actions to avoid problems.

The major problem in this position is that you are required to double up your position in the stock. And you might not want to double up. What if the stock continues to fall? What if you don't have the money available or the margin credit? For any number of reasons, you might not want to double up on this particular stock; but at the same time, you don't want to be out of the market for more than 30 days just to avoid a wash sale. What can you do?

Consider what I like to call the "Thanksgiving-Christmas-Super Bowl Spread." For example, say you originally bought 100 shares at $65 and they fell to $35. This is a dilemma. You would like to continue to be invested long-term, but you also want to take that loss this year. Table 7.2 summarizes the solution to this problem.

One drawback to buying more shares is that it requires more money—and given that the stock's value has fallen, that is not always a wise move.

Here I propose buying one of the January '10 30 strike LEAPS calls at $8.50. Now I own 100 shares on which I would like to take a current-year loss, rather than buying another 100 shares at $35. This alternative costs less than one-fourth as well, $850 versus $3,500.

Table 7.2 · The Thanksgiving-Christmas-Super Bowl Spread	
November 24th ('08)	Buy 1 XYZ Jan '10 30 strike LEAPS call at $8.50
December 26th ('08)	Sell 100 shares of XYZ at $35
Jan 29th or 30th (a choice)	Continue to own the LEAPS call for the next 11 ½ months
	Buy 100 shares and sell the LEAPS call, reestablishing the original position

On December 26, I sell my 100 shares at $35, or whatever the current price might be, and set up my net loss on the stock for the year. Now, I do have risk owning stock and owning a LEAPS call for 31 days or more. I did "double up" for a short period of time, but with a LEAPS call, not more shares. On January 31, the "Super Bowl" portion of this strategy, I can either do nothing for almost another year, or I can sell the long LEAPS call and buy back the stock at $35 (assuming the stock does not move).

This is a valid approach as long as the stock is worth more than $30 per share. If the stock were to be sharply lower and I was still bullish, I could also consider buying 100 shares and continue holding the LEAPS call. I would control 200 shares and have cash left over.

> You can use LEAPS long positions to avoid the usual problems of year-end strategies. Cost is lower than buying more shares and time decay is minimal.

GETTING BACK INTO THE LONG STOCK POSITION

This strategy got me out of the 30-day period on each side of that December 26 starting date. As you see at the bottom of Table 7.2, on January 29 or 30, I can reestablish the original position by replacing the LEAPS call with 100 shares, placing me back where I started. The only thing that has changed in this strategy is that I got my tax loss.

I think this is a very interesting strategy to consider if you're trying to create a tax loss this year without doubling up or staying out of the market. You might have the Santa Claus rally, the January effect, and the Super Bowl rally, all within the period in question. Going with the traditional approach of staying out of the market more than 30 days means you could lose opportunities to profit. This strategy lets you double up at a very reduced cost.

Many rallying opportunities may occur in December and January, so covering your bases with the LEAPS strategy helps avoid lost opportunity risk.

As far as the tax ramifications are concerned, the IRS does not limit how far in-the-money that LEAPS call can be. The only restrictions, so-called "qualified calls," involve short calls out-of-the-money. And as far as the wash rule is concerned, the strategy is set up to make sure the LEAPS purchase is more than 30 days before I sell the stock.

Taking a loss on your stock opens up possible tax implications, even when you avoid the 30-day restriction. For example, you're only allowed to claim losses up to $3,000 per year. So if your overall net loss is higher, you have to carry over the excess to next year. This kind of year-end tax strategy works best when you have net gains, because the loss reduces your tax on these other gains.

Another advantage is that this keeps you in the market, so if the stock rallies, you don't lose out. No one wants to exchange a tax loss for a missed opportunity, and this strategy covers both.

Table 7.3 - Year-End LEAPS Tax Strategy - Pros and Cons	
Pros	Realize loss on stock
	Still in the market with minimal outlay and limited risk
Cons	Somewhat commission intensive
	Amount invested in LEAPS as well as amount invested in stock at risk for first 31 days

Disadvantages include transaction costs. This is a somewhat commission intensive strategy. You're buying the LEAPS, selling the stock, and then possibly reversing the positions. That's a lot of commission. Of course, if you're using an online discount broker, that's really a minor consideration these days, but cost should always be in the mix when you're weighing the pros and cons of any strategy.

Even if you claim a large year-end loss, you cannot deduct more than $3,000 on overall net positions each year. So if you have losses above that level, a year-end strategy to claim more losses would have to be rolled into future years.

Another disadvantage is that during the first 31 days of this multi-tiered strategy, you are at risk for both the stock and the LEAPS long positions. If the values fall, you have doubled your risk with these positions. So the tax write-off has to be worth the risk, a judgment call on your part.

Table 7.4 - **LEAPS Summary**
• Wide range of possible uses
• Can be a strategic tool for risk management
• Can help combat one of the greatest enemies of options buyers: TIME EROSION

Table 7.3 and Table 7.4 summarize the pros and cons of this year-end strategy.

FLEXIBILITY IN YEAR-END STRATEGIES

There is certainly a wide range of uses for LEAPS year-end strategies. The nice thing about this strategy is that it can be tweaked in a number of ways. If you think of the LEAPS at year-end as a strategic tool of risk management, you can avoid opportunity loss by being out of the market, take a tax loss, and keep your exposure to a minimum.

Remember, the primary purpose in using this LEAPS year-end strategy is to maximize potential while reducing loss or market risk.

Most important, this strategy helps avoid one of the greatest enemies for all option buyers: time erosion. Time erosion on long-term LEAPS options is far less than that on short-term options. That's why I like this particular approach using the LEAPS call. It's initially more expensive than buying a short-term option because of the time value, but with relatively small time erosion and a limited number of days of exposure, it is often the most rational way to get this protection.

> Time works against long option positions, but it is advantageous if you are short. However, if you are short and you want fast decay, short-term options work better.

If I sell an option, I'd like to have it fall off the face of the earth a little quicker. If I own an option, I'd like to give myself more time. That's the big difference between longer and shorter dated options.

FLEXIBILITY FOR LARGER PORTFOLIOS

Another consideration comes into play if you have a large portfolio. Rather than selling an index call option, I'd prefer to sell 10 individual stock options and collect 10 premiums as opposed to collecting only one premium. The advantage to collecting one premium is that it requires only one commission. The disadvantage of selling 10 premiums is 10 commissions. But if I'm a seller of options in an index, I'd rather take a look at my current holdings and sell out-of-the-money options on those individual stocks—especially if I don't think they're going to be off to the races in the short term.

One of the problems with LEAPS is the bid/ask spread. You might see where a particular LEAPS has a $21 bid—offered at $21.50. These long-term contracts are not like the shorter-term options where you might see a $2 bid offered at $2.05. The LEAPS options are not as liquid. If we're buying the offer on the way in (initiating a long position) and selling the bid on the way out, we're giving up a bit of an edge.

> The spread is a hidden cost in the LEAPS trade. Add the spread to your other transaction costs to get a realistic picture of your total costs.

LEAPS are probably not efficient products to trade in short-term time increments for this reason. If you're the type of trader who buys on Monday and sells on Wednesday, LEAPS are probably not the most efficient product for you. They are long-term securities. People who invest in LEAPS positions usually leave them on for a while.

The question often comes up as to how LEAPS transactions are reported to the IRS. You are required to file capital gains on your tax return, including LEAPS capital gains and losses. As to how you report your LEAPS transactions, remember one easy rule: anytime you sell an option, even if it's a LEAPS, it's a short-term capital gain or loss. If you sell a two-year option and you wait 12 months, you have not established a holding period because you never owned the option. If you own a LEAPS for more than 12 months, the tax considerations can change significantly.

The *Taxes and Investing* document can be downloaded very easily. I suggest sharing this with your tax advisor.

To learn how the professionals buy and sell LEAPS calls, visit www.traderslibrary.com/TLEcorner.

Taxes & Investing

For comprehensive information on option taxes, contact any one of the exchanges for a FREE copy of the booklet *Taxes and Investing: A Guide for the Individual Investor*. You can also download it at http://www.cboe.com/LearnCenter/pdf/TaxesandInvesting.pdf or call The Options Industry Council at 1-888-OPTIONS. It covers almost every scenario you can think of as to how taxes work on various option strategies.

1. When you own stock that has gone down in value:

   a. you might as well hold and wait because you are not allowed to deduct net losses.

   b. you should sell on December 31 and repurchase on January 1 to get a loss in the current year.

   c. you can sell, but you have to wait more than 30 days before you can repurchase.

   d. the only solution is to buy more shares to average down your basis in the stock.

2. The "wash sale" rule states that:

   a. if you sell and then repurchase with 30 days before or after the sale, the sale cannot be counted as a tax loss.

   b. you have to be able to document the source of funds used to avoid charges of money laundering.

   c. a long stock position and a short LEAPS position offsetting one another are a wash and don't affect profit or loss.

   d. you can only deduct losses on short option positions, not on any long positions.

3. One way to get around the year-end restrictions on loss deductions is to:

    a.   sell 100 shares in early December to claim a loss, but repurchase before the end of the year.

    b.   buy an additional 100 shares in November and then sell the original 100 shares more than 30 days later, but before December 31.

    c.   wait until January 1 before taking any action.

    d.   take the loss only if you have offsetting investment gains.

4. An important tax rule to remember is:

    a.   you are taxed at a lower rate for long-term capital gains.

    b.   you can deduct no more than $3,000 per year in net capital losses.

    c.   all LEAPS transactions have to be reported on your tax return.

    d.   all of the above.

5. The Thanksgiving-Christmas-Super Bowl spread is called such because:

   a. the actions involved can only be done within one week of each of the named events.
   b. the typical timing for each phase of the strategy requires 30+ days to work.
   c. it is illegal to enter spreads outside of the November-to-January window.
   d. everyone is so busy during the holiday season that they ignore market opportunities.

For answers, go to www.traderslibrary.com/TLEcorner.

Glossary

American style option—an option that can be exercised at any time by the owner of the call or put. All stock (equity) options and all ETF options (including LEAPS on those) are American style options. Some index options are American style.

Annualized return—any return from an investment, calculated as though the position were open for exactly one year (for example, a three-month position's return would be multiplied by four to annualize; and a two-year position would be divided by two).

Assignment—the seller of an option is notified that they were assigned when an owner of the option exercised their right to do so. For every option exercised, someone is assigned.

At-the-money (ATM)—status of any option when the stock value is closest to the strike price.

Call—an option granting its owner the right, but not the obligation, to buy 100 shares of an underlying security, at a fixed price before expiration.

Capital gains—the gains on investment activity, which are taxed based on the holding period.

Carryover loss—the net capital losses in excess of $3,000, which must be used in future tax years.

Collar—an option strategy with three parts: ownership of stock, a covered call, and a long put purchased with the call proceeds.

Conversion security—descriptive of a LEAPS option, which may be converted to the purchase or sale of stock; or that will be converted to an option when expiration will occur in less than nine months. This term is used infrequently.

Covered call—a short call, written by an investor who also owns 100 shares of the underlying security for each call written.

Delta—The relationship of price movement between options and their underlying security. If the underlying moves one point, a .50 delta option should move about $0.50. Delta changes as the underlying moves higher or lower and as expiration approaches.

European style option—an option that can be exercised only in a brief window of time, normally limited to the one day prior to expiration. Most index options are European.

Exchange-traded fund (ETF)—a type of mutual fund with an unchanging basket of securities, traded on exchanges like stocks and often available for option trading.

Exercise—the act of calling shares away by a call owner, or putting shares to a seller of a put.

Expiration—the month and day on which an option becomes worthless, typically the Saturday following the third Friday of a specified expiration month; or the quarterly cycle on which a series of options is scheduled to expire.

In-the-money (ITM)—status of a call option when stock price is higher than strike; or of a put option when the stock price is lower than the strike.

Intrinsic value—that portion of an option's premium value equal to the number of points the option is in-the-money.

LEAPS—Long-term Equity AnticiPation Securities; options with active lives in excess of the nine-month life span associated with traditional listed options.

Listed option—a traditional option with a maximum life no greater than nine months.

Long-term capital gains—any investment gains on positions left open for 12 months or longer (some option positions are exceptions to this rule, and are treated as short-term regardless of the holding period).

Married put—a position involving the purchase of stock and of a put on the stock.

Naked call—alternate name for an uncovered call.

Out-of-the-money (OTM)—status of a call option when stock price is lower than strike; or of a put option when the stock price is higher than the strike.

Premium—the value of an option, expressed on a per-share basis; because options refer to 100 shares, the premium has to be converted to a dollar value 100 times greater (thus, premium of 4.50 is equal to $450).

Protective put—a put purchased to protect the risk of loss on stock owned by an investor, due to a price decline in the underlying shares. Think of protective puts as an insurance policy on stock.

Put—an option granting its owner the right, but not the obligation, to sell 100 shares of an underlying security, at a fixed price before expiration.

Qualified call—a short call within a specified in-the-money range, which allows the investor to take advantage of long-term capital gains rates on the underlying stock (unqualified covered calls eliminate the counting period for long-term capital gains qualification).

Short-term capital gains—any investment gains on positions left open for less than 12 months.

Spread—a strategy involving two positions. An option spread, for example, might be a short call with a strike above the current value of the underlying, coupled with a long call with a strike below the current value. This spread example would be known as a bullish call debit spread.

Strike price—the price per share at which options may be exercised, regardless of the current market value of the underlying stock. This is also known as the exercise price.

Synthetic call—owning shares of stock and a protective put would be an example of a synthetic call.

Time value—the portion of an option or LEAPS premium beyond any intrinsic value, representing the time element; time value is greater when there is more time until expiration and will decay as expiration approaches.

Uncovered call—a short call written when the writer does not also own 100 shares of the underlying security.

Underlying security—the stock on which options may be bought or sold.

Wash sale rule—a tax rule specifying that a loss cannot be deducted in the current year if an offsetting transaction in the same position occurs within 30 days before or after the sale date.

Printed and bound by CPI Group (UK) Ltd, Croydon, CR0 4YY

16/04/2025

14658522-0005